PORTRAIT OF CANTERBURY

Portrait of
CANTERBURY

JOHN BOYLE

ROBERT HALE · LONDON

© John Boyle 1974
First published in Great Britain 1974

ISBN 0 7091 4344 3

Robert Hale & Company
63 Old Brompton Road
London, S.W.7

PRINTED IN GREAT BRITAIN
BY EBENEZER BAYLIS AND SON, LIMITED
THE TRINITY PRESS, WORCESTER, AND LONDON

CONTENTS

ACKNOWLEDGEMENTS

My friends Christopher Gay, Frank Higenbottam and John Berbiers, and their staffs, have given me quite invaluable help in writing and illustrating this book.

As these words are written they (my friends that is) are respectively the Town Clerk, City Librarian and City Architect of Canterbury. What position they may occupy by the time this acknowledgement is published is quite another question—one which, being denied the gift of prophecy, I cannot completely answer.

I certainly wish them well in a future that the reorganisation of local government has made uncertain, if not entirely unhopeful.

Another friend, James Martin, Principal of the Canterbury College of Art has just given me a copy of the handsomely illustrated *Selection of the Miracles of St. Thomas of Canterbury* produced by the College Press with the assistance of the King's School, Canterbury. The existence of this volume disproves what I say in the chapter on Becket, about there being no modern book giving the details of the miracles, but largely confirms what I have written about the nature of them.

The extracts from *Murder in the Cathedral* by T. S. Eliot are printed by courtesy of Messrs Faber and Faber.

Finally, there are many others who have answered my questions and helped me in divers ways; to them I express my gratitude.

ILLUSTRATIONS

facing page

PLANS

PICTURE CREDITS

W. L. Entwistle, Canterbury: 10, 13, 17, 18, 19, 21, 22, 30,
31; Airviews Ltd., Manchester: 15; *Kent Messenger*: 20;
remainder: Ben May, Canterbury.

PRELIMINARY

PORTRAITS

THERE are portraits and portraits. To see the truth of this one needs only refer to the many examples that Canterbury itself can provide. Some of them present good likenesses; some are great works of art; some portray famous subjects. And some, in each case, do not.

The aisles, colonnades and side-chapels of the cathedral are the setting for innumerable recumbent effigies in stone, brass, or even wood and plaster, of archbishops, kings, queens, warriors, and other great and worthy men and women; while its windows—twelfth-century precursors of colour television—display in painted glass the generations of man from Adam, the many saints of the mediaeval church, and royal personages from the Yorkist victors of the Roses' War to Queen Victoria and our present royal family.

Elsewhere too the city has an ample stock of portraits in oils—in the municipal art gallery, in college halls and schools, and in private houses.

In the mayor's quarters are hung the likenesses of local worthies—mayors, aldermen and benefactors—from the time of Queen Elizabeth I onward. When this collection was shown to an expert from the National Portrait Gallery, he reported, '. . . none is of any great artistic merit . . . Despite this I congratulate the Corporation on having preserved so many portraits of worthies of Canterbury over the past four hundred years . . . Despite their lack of any great merit, skilful cleaning would, I believe, make them worthy decorations of the city's civic buildings.'

This opinion is of some comfort to a writer approaching with some diffidence the task of painting in words a Portrait of Canterbury. He may hope that the inherent interest of the subject-matter will amply compensate for the deficiencies of the artist. And he can at least see to it that no 'cleaning' is required before publication.

MEN, NOT WALLS...

'Men, not walls, make a city.' One remembers uneasily the old tag—Thucydides, wasn't it?—quoting some apocryphal speech of an Athenian general. Across the centuries he sounds a warning that writers must heed when they try to portray cities. Must not the old, dead walls, and all that goes with them, yield pride of place, he seems to say, to the men and women of the modern bustling community?

In Canterbury, if we are to study men rather than walls, the time to see people in their thousands is a weekday afternoon in summer, and as good a place as any, the Parade—that short stretch of the ancient main street so named because, of old, the militia drilled there. Standing near the tailor's shop that looks across rather smugly to see the Longmarket curving gently from the Parade to Burgate, the student of humanity will never find himself short of material; but he must hold fast to Thucydides' warning, otherwise his attention might be diverted to the Longmarket, where splashes of saffron and scarlet from summer flowers and delicate screens of birch leaves soften so attractively the crispness of the modern architecture. He must certainly avert his gaze from Bell Harry,[1] from clustered pinnacles thrusting upward to the flawless azure of a Kentish sky, from those grey stones dazzlingly whitened by the flattery of the summer sun, from buttress, embrasure and moulding that etch in shadows the sculptured detail of that matchless tower.

It is hard to describe a modern scene without using some of the hideous jargon of the planners and architects of the present time; by now everyone knows what is meant by these terms, and if ever they had purer synonyms, everyone has forgotten them. One such expression is 'pedestrian precinct', and this is precisely what the Longmarket is. The pedestrians circulate between small bright shops, and the monotony of the pavement they tread is broken by patterns of granite sets and varied by cobbles. A tower block prevents the profile from sagging, and is deliberately made stark and modern so as not to compete impertinently with the

[1] Bell Harry is the central tower of the cathedral, too well-known in Canterbury to need further description.

exquisite beauty of Bell Harry. Dramatic contrast is achieved
between the great cathedral tower and the modern foreground,
with its television emporia, shoe shops and jewellers' boutiques;
and the historian can amuse himself by creating similar contrasts
between the men who traded in this part of Canterbury centuries
ago—Terric the Goldsmith in mediaeval times and Richard
Marlowe the shoemaker, father of the playwright, in the days of
Queen Elizabeth I—and their modern counterparts.

South-east from the Longmarket, the main street mutates from
the Parade to St. George's Street at a point better known to the
postman than to the general public, and here, using more
developers' jargon, is the cream shopping area where the multiples
congregate, the Woolworths and the Marks and Spencers and all
the other shops whose names are household words and whose
branches appear in every High Street of any note throughout the
country.

On the pavements the throng is enormous. Who are these
people, and what are they doing? Where are they going to and
where are they coming from? The faces of most of them have a
determined, serious, but tolerant look because they are English
and adult. More light-hearted are some of the foreigners,
especially the French, and the younger people. Women tend to
predominate, and there is a sprinkling of retired couples, many of
whom have a tan that is too deep to have come from the temper-
ate suns of England. An occasional young executive bustles along
in an immaculate light-weight business suit; a public schoolboy
ambles past in pinstripe pants and straw hat, rubbing shoulders
with an unimaginable scarecrow of indeterminate sex and
personal habits, swathed in an army jacket dyed magenta.
Between these limits the crowds display a varied spectrum of
styles of attire.

So far there has not been very much to be learnt about the feel
of Canterbury from going amongst its citizens. All we have here
is pushing and bustle, and men and women, apart from the
foreigners and the occasional student, little different from those
of any other English town.

The attempt to study the humanity of Canterbury might
perhaps be more usefully continued where there is less of a crush
—Mercery Lane and Sun Street, for instance. The former, a
narrow cleft between oversailing mediaeval houses, leads straight
to the Christchurch Gateway, where the tourists' cameras click

incessantly. The lane is shaded by the enclosing buildings and unbelievably picturesque with the gay and gilded heraldry painted on the stones of the gatehouse screening the far end; and, above and beyond, the pinnacles of the cathedral's western towers form a second screen which sinks gradually from view behind the gateway as one approaches it. The narrow lane is left behind to reveal on the right, suddenly and dramatically, the intimate little square of the old Buttermarket, and the spires of Bell Harry from a new angle, while on the left, little wider than Mercery Lane itself, is Sun Street, called after 'The Sun Inn', onetime alleged haunt of Wilkins Micawber. The crowds here are only slightly less dense than the hurrying throngs on the Parade and in St. George's Street, but by pleasant contrast they are strolling, or standing and looking and taking photographs, or peacefully drinking beer under the colourful umbrellas outside the public house in the corner of the Buttermarket.

Through the Christchurch Gateway into the precincts of the cathedral there flows a broad and continuous stream of humanity to and from the south-east porch of the cathedral some fifty yards away. Parties of Americans mix with crocodiles of schoolchildren in uniform blazers clutching guide books, and even the occasional clergyman, and there are for the rest tourists, the same sort of people that you will find at this time of the year milling round in the Piazza San Marco, the Champs Elysées or the Tower of London.

Are there denizens more distinctive of the city in other parts? At the great concrete complex of hospitals in south Canterbury? At the world-famous county cricket ground just near it, up at the half-deserted barracks, on the windy campus of the university overlooking the city from its northern hill, at the teeming weekly open-air market at St. Stephen's? Without going to all these places we know the answer. All the bustle and modern activity, welcome no doubt to the city's traders and caterers, can scarcely be said to be characteristic of Canterbury. What are they but a foil to the ancient and mystical charm of the place? And the tourists streaming to and from the cathedral have come from afar, to gaze at the very Canterbury we are trying to portray.

Perhaps Thucydides has unwittingly led us astray; after all we did take him out of context, and his approach is perchance too modern for us, like that of many ancient Greek writers. At this stage we remember some words of a great Englishman who spent his last years in this very county of Kent. He was a greater warrior than any Athenian general (except possibly the victor of Marathon) and could certainly compete with Thucydides as an historian. 'It is only by studying the past,' growled Churchill, 'that we can understand, however dimly, the present.'

We must start again; this time at the museum, amongst the prehistoric stone axes.

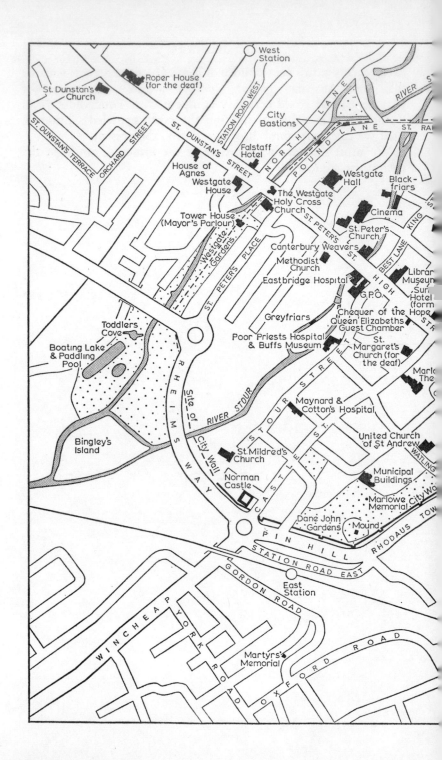

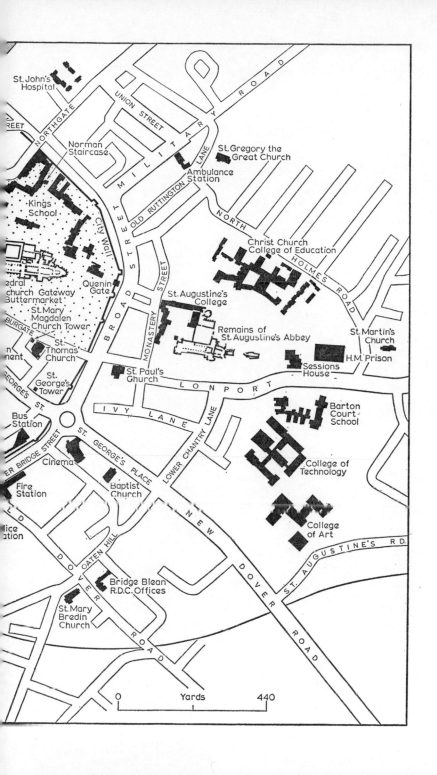

St. John's
Hospital

NORTHGATE

UNION STREET

MILITARY ROAD

Norman
Staircase

OLD RUTTINGTON LANE

St. Gregory the
Great Church

Ambulance
Station

CITY WALL

BROAD STREET

STREET

NORTH HOLMES ROAD

Christ Church
College of Education

Kings
School

Quenin
Gate

MONASTERY STREET

St. Augustine's
College

St. Martin's
Church

dral
church Gateway
Buttermarket

St. Mary
Magdalen
Church Tower

Remains of
St. Augustine's Abbey

H.M. Prison

BURGATE

St.
Thomas'
Church

St. Paul's
Church

Sessions
House

nt

GEORGES ST.

St.
George's
Tower

IVY LANE

LONPORT

LOWER CHANTRY LANE

Barton
Court
School

Bus
Station

ER BRIDGE STREET

ST. GEORGE'S PLACE

College of
Technology

Cinema

Fire
Station

Baptist
Church

NEW

DOVER

ST. AUGUSTINE'S RD.

College
of Art

ice
ation

OATEN HILL

Bridge Blean
R.D.C. Offices

DOVER ROAD

ST. AUGUSTINE'S ROAD

St. Mary
Bredin
Church

0   Yards   440

ONE

AT THE BEANEY

WHERE, then, does Canterbury keep its prehistoric stone axes? You have only to ask anyone in the street, and unless they are complete strangers—or completely dumb—they will give you the answer:

'At the Beaney!'

And where is 'the Beaney?' Within a couple of hundred yards of the Christchurch Gateway, but in the most commercialised and the most Victorian of the old streets that escaped destruction during the war, in 1942. High Street has its share of ancient buildings and reminders of the past—the small fragment of the pilgrims' hostel at the corner of Mercery Lane, the ambitiously-named Queen Elizabeth's Guest Chamber, the little rest garden on the site of St. Mary Bredman's Church—and a rather jolly nineteenth-century Cardinal-Wolsey-style Bank, but it has also a great deal of nondescript recent stuff; and notably it has the building that Canterbury calls 'the Beaney.'

Architecturally, few would claim that the Royal Museum and Beaney Institute, to give it its full title, is an asset to the city. An ornate pseudo-Tudor structure, with hints of Scotch baronial, it has pink tessellated panels between the decorative timbers to give a reminder, presumably, of ancient Rome. Hercule Poirot, one feels, with his passion for strict symmetry and his waxed-moustache fixation, would have found it *formidable*; on principle Sir John Betjeman probably adores it; but to the ordinary person, the building seems unpleasantly overbearing, completely out-of-scale with its neighbours, and foreign to the quiet, urbane character of Canterbury's better buildings.

Poirot, by the way, and his creator Miss Agatha Christie, are by no means unknown to those who frequent the Beaney; its ground floor is the public library. Archaeology (together with natural history, art, and that sort of thing) is upstairs.

To account for the name of the building we have to go back to the reign of good Queen Victoria when there was in Canterbury a boy named James George Beaney who decided that when he grew up he would like to be a doctor. He took his training at Guy's Hospital and Edinburgh and, duly qualified, embarked on the career of a country doctor in the west of England, as his wife came from those parts. He decided to try his luck in Australia, and rarely has a gamble turned out better. His success was immediate; everyone seemed to like and respect Dr. Beaney, and he proceeded to amass a vast fortune without forfeiting their regard, which appears greatly to his credit; nor did his good fortune cause him to forget his ties with England and with Canterbury. It is painful to record that he was sometimes in legal trouble, but he was always vindicated in court, and with each vindication his success and his popularity grew. Now Dr. Beaney left the greater part of his fortune for public and charitable purposes, including £10,000 to the Corporation of the City of Canterbury to provide a mechanics' institute and a public reading room, to which, in the event, a museum was added; through further slight metamorphoses, the building has continued to bear the testator's name. Dr. Beaney was no Becket or Anselm; just a successful doctor, but there are thousands of Canterburians to whom his name means more than that of any archbishop that ever was, because it comes into their daily round, and they let it slip off their tongues almost without thinking. 'The Beaney': in a way, just as much a part of the essential Canterbury as Bell Harry or the Westgate.

But we digress, as one does so often in this interesting city; we were looking really for the museum. On the wall above the dreary pink concrete steps with their ponderous balustrade, that lead to the first floor, is a massive plaque, rescued when the Canterbury Festival Exhibition of 1951 was dismantled. In faultless College of Art Trajanic lettering is the following bold claim written in 1540 by John Twyne:

Nulla paene civitas huius regni, vel natalium antiquitate, vel fortunae dignitate, huic nostae preferenda aut ne cum hac quidem sit conferenda.

(Scarce any city of this realm is there to be preferred to this of ours in antiquity of origin or in dignity of fortune, or for that matter, to be compared with her.)

Twyne was Mayor of Canterbury, and we shall be hearing more about him in due course.

The museum does its best to live up to this impressive introduction; the large scale of the building does at least provide lofty galleries; money and skill have been lavished on the displays, and there is no shortage of material. Our palaeolithic and neolithic implements are there in various shapes and sizes; for the classical enthusiast there is Samian in plenty (the shiny red table ware imported not from Samos but from Gaul, in that hopeful time when people were plumping for the better life that Roman civilisation meant). Trinkets and glass from Jutish graves, and coins from the mints that produced the first penny in history, fill in the Saxon period. Rugged looking mediaeval pitchers, a tithe of those the Beaney holds in its keeping, evoke thoughts of sack and mead, and thirsty men-at-arms fresh home from Continental wars.

All this is part of the unending epic of Canterbury, recorded in the loams and brickearths that underlie the city, and in the broken ruins, pits and graves that abound, often unsuspected, beneath its surface. The story is spelt out in a language often unintelligible except to the archaeologist, and translated for us in his reports. To him these pots and tools and trinkets are, most of the time, mere dating material, of no more scientific interest than the humblest potsherd that he can as easily identify.

The most highly prized of the museum's archaeological possessions was found by sheer accident by workmen, and has its own little showcase in the middle of the gallery—the hoard of Romano-British silver spoons. They were hidden, it is safe to say, about A.D. 400 by a thoroughly frightened man, at night, when the distant skies were red with the glow of burning villas, and Roman Britain was in course of disintegration. He never returned.

But archaeology by itself can tell only part of the tale. The natural history gallery has something to say about the causes, as distinct from the effects of man's activity in Canterbury and its neighbourhood. One can begin with the relief model of Kent, which shows where Canterbury stands; a short distance inland, with easy access to various creeks and harbours on three sides, while keeping guard over the entrance to the highly strategic gap in the North Downs made by the valley of the Stour.

Hundreds of thousands of years ago the Stour was not the tiny trickle of a trout stream that it is today, but a mighty, swampy river a mile or two wide. At Chartham, at the turn of the seventeenth century, the enormous bones of some prehistoric beast were unearthed, and the savants of the time debated whether these had belonged to some species of mammoth or to a hippopotamus. It may well be that primeval changes in the temperature enabled both these beasts, at different times, to wallow in the morasses of the Stour valley. Several feet of sluggish water covered the place where the city and cathedral were to rise; where preachers were to reconcile divine omnipotence with the existence of evil, eels wriggled and dodged about; where property-developers were to be satisfied with their fifteen per cent (excluding on-costs) the hungry pike snatched at his prey. A little higher, where the parishioners of St. Stephen's grow their roses, the gravel terraces were formed that occasionally produce those pear-shaped artefacts made from nodules of flint by palaeolithic man.

These implements have been lying around for anything up to 300,000 years and are the oldest man-made objects to be found in the city, or, apart from the dubious 'eoliths' (which are so dubious in fact that they really do not count) anywhere else, for that matter. Canterbury's time-scale, therefore, covers the whole period of rational human existence.

But, say the archaeologists, these flints have come 'from another horizon,' brought here by the river; they do not prove that there was any settlement at Canterbury. This is true enough, and in fact the people who used these axes do not seem to have settled anywhere, except possibly in caves, of which Canterbury is destitute. The first steps towards *settlement* were taken a couple of hundred thousand years later by neolithic man, who was more 'neo' than 'lithic'; although he used 'lithos'—stone—he was a farmer, a weaver and a potter, unlike his palaeolithic predecessor who was little more than a skin-clad wandering animal with a few cunning monkey tricks with sharpened flints.

Undoubted traces of neolithic occupation have been found in the city, near the river; the fact is that as soon as civilisation started in Britain, Canterbury started. If you study the map of prehistoric Britain it will show you why. These early men were not exactly well equipped for clearing forests and draining bogs; bulldozers and trenching machines were yet to be invented so the inhabitants had to take the country as they found it and use for travel as well as living those parts that nature had obligingly left dry and free from large immoveable trees, which in practice meant downland, wold land and limestone ridges. Many tracts of this kind radiate from Salisbury Plain, which itself is one of the areas that prehistoric man would have regarded as eminently suitable for development.

So the Plain was thickly populated, perhaps not as thickly as London or Manchester are today, but well covered by the standards of those times, and Stonehenge and Avebury were the St. Paul's Cathedral and the Piccadilly Circus of the prehistoric metropolis. One of the trackways that radiated from this central nucleus was the system of uplands represented by the Hog's Back and the North Downs. Just as, today, trains leave Charing Cross bound for Canterbury and Dover so, three thousand years ago, travellers left Salisbury Plain for the same destinations, and for the latter part of their journey followed the same approximate route.

On the map of modern Kent, various odd lengths of road are labelled 'Pilgrims' Way.' These bits of road follow the Downs; not the route of Chaucer's pilgrims, who came straight from London; they are older than Christianity itself, and have nothing specifically to do with pilgrims at all. Through Winchester, Farnham and the Hog's Back the trail led to the North Downs, Canterbury and eventually to Dover. From Farnham onward at least it can still be traced, whether as a lane, as a bridle path or cart track, or only as a fieldside footpath or a mere row of trees.

Until it got to the valley of the Stour the trackway ran along the south face of the Downs, but the obstacle forced the trail to veer north-eastward in the direction of the place where Canterbury now stands. How was this cut through the Downs, so clearly important in the early history of the city, formed? By the geological process known as 'borrowing' by a river; at first there would be two rivers flowing from the high ground in opposite directions, but the Stour, augmented by downpours of the kind that in later eons were to wash out cricket matches and anniversary celebrations, developed into a foaming cataract that bit deeper and deeper into the chalk until it began to tap the headwaters of the other river, finally appropriating it altogether, and reversing its flow. So the Downs were cut, and the ground was prepared for Canterbury's entry into prehistory as the place where the trunk route from Salisbury Plain (where the action then was) to Dover (then as now the main port for the Continent) crossed the River Stour.

The geological processes took millions of years, but once man appeared on the scene the pace quickened; fundamental changes took only a few hundred thousand years, then thousands, and in the end centuries only separated the different eras such as the Neolithic and Bronze Ages, with a sort of mixture of the two in between.

Bronze Age objects have been found in Canterbury, but what is technically called their provenance (i.e. where they were found) has not been recorded except in the vaguest terms, such as 'near Sturry Road.' They are accordingly of little value archaeologically. It is only when we get to the early Iron Age that there is an occupied site to record. In the 1950s local people investigated a bombed site at the corner of Castle Street and St. John's Lane, now occupied by a small car park. Beneath the modern surface a forest of small post-holes, three or four inches in diameter, penetrated the clay loam. The excited diggers then discovered larger post-holes, nine inches in diameter, going down several feet into the clay, the empty sockets having large tangs (like the barb that fish hooks have) at the bottom end, and halo-like rings in the surrounding loam showed the chemical effect of the rotting away of wood. Crude potsherds abounded, and the post-holes turned out to be those of a palisade in front of which was a large ditch. The experts have decided that the pottery, from which it was possible to reconstruct one crudely made urn, dates from somewhere between 350 and 250 B.C. Now who were the people who made this fortification and this pot? Before the Romans came, Britain was invaded with monotonous regularity by peoples who could not write and left no recorded history, so that we have no way of knowing what they called themselves and archaeologists have had the inconvenience of inventing names for them. The two main sources of nomenclature were objects that a civilisation used, or the place where their culture was first identified. From the use of the first method we hear of Beaker folk, the Urn people, Battle-axe men, Food Vessel culture; from the use of the second the Abbevillean, Acheulian and Mousterian cultures, and nearer home the Creswellian Cavemen, the Cromer flake people, and the Clactonian folk.

Why should Cromer, Cresswell and even it seems Clacton, have all the honour and glory? As traces of an important settlement have been found in Canterbury, of a period when peoples were named after the modern places where their remains have been found, it seems only right that we should now add to the list the Castle Street culture—or would it be better to speak of the St. John's Lane car park people? Whatever the nomenclature, the fact is that this city, so richly endowed with history from the beginning of the Christian era to the present time, can now carry its story back two, if not three, centuries into prehistory.

From the time of the Castle Street settlement, there is a long gap during which little or nothing is known about events at Canterbury; the period of ignorance is terminated by the arrival on the coast of Kent of Julius Caesar and his legions, in 55 B.C. By acting as his own war correspondent Caesar managed to hide from the Roman public the fact that his first expedition to Britain was a complete fiasco, and that on the second, although he took a much bigger army and fleet, he failed to achieve his objective which, though he did not admit it, was undoubtedly the conquest of Britain. Within this strategic failure however war correspondent Caesar was able to report a number of tactical successes, one of which was the conquest of Bigberry, a British camp two miles west of Canterbury. The mysterious and puzzling system of earthworks which exists today would have been supplemented by palisades and felled trees, but it gave the legionaries no trouble; they locked their shields, and went up the rampart and through the defences before you could say 'Cassivellaunus'.

Caesar describes the Britons as being fierce, flesh-eating, skin-clothed savages; when the archaeological evidence shows that they have left behind jewellery more tasteful and artistic than that of the Romans, a coinage of gold, silver, bronze and tin, and evidence of agricultural pursuits, expert manufacture of pottery, and weaving of garments. No doubt it suited Caesar's book to tell the rebellious Gauls and the people at home in Italy a story of the fierce, bloodthirsty warriors whom he had overcome.

To get rid of Caesar the Britons had to agree to pay tribute to Rome, but never did so; for all that, the Romans left them alone for nearly a hundred years, and it was not until A.D. 43 that the Emperor Claudius, either wanting a cheap triumph or, as Tacitus had been told, having learnt of pearl-bearing oysters to be found in Britain, decided to stage a full-scale invasion. By this time there had been big changes at Canterbury.

The oppidum at Bigberry had been more like a corral than a place for men and women to live. After Julius Caesar had retired with, as the Britons no doubt thought, a bloody nose, the East

Kent Belgae began to wonder why the cattle should be the only creatures to enjoy the benefits of an organised settlement, could think of no valid reason, and moved, with all their women, goods and chattels, a couple of miles down the trackway to comfortable quarters beside the Stour. The deserted palisades of the Castle Street folk and the long-used ford were excellent landmarks. The men got their backs into it and in no time at all there was an imposing conglomeration of round huts, neatly thatched and well finished off with plaster walls—no self-respecting Belga would have assented to the use of the archaeologists' term 'daub'— which they named Durwhern.

This was probably the one time in Canterbury's history when everyone was happy and content. With fresh water from the river, grain in the storage jars, from the fertile lowland fields, and trout for dinner, what more could anyone want? All the inhabitants of southern Britain at this time were, as is well known, Celts, people who later invaders called 'Welsh'. Did they speak, one wonders, *Yr hen iaith*? In the invigorating air of a spring morning did the good ladies walk the alleys of Durwhern, attired in their beautifully woven cloaks pinned by tasteful La Tene jewellery, while exchanging such remarks as, *'Bore da; mae'n braf heddiw!'* *'Sut mae. Go dda, diolch.'* And were there protests against the new-fangled coinage with the names of the local king, Vosenos, and his overlord Cunobelin in *Roman* letters?

Claudius's invading troops landed in overwhelming force at Rutupiae (Richborough, near Sandwich), and were successful largely because reconnaissance, better than Caesar had been able to carry out, had discovered a safe and sheltered harbour for the transports. A fort was built to cover the disembarcation, and after consolidating their positions the legions fanned out and quickly occupied all of south-east Britain. Although Durwhern— Durovernum as we must now call it—was on the route from Richborough to London, and was to become an important junction of Roman roads, we do not hear of any fighting in the neighbourhood of the city, except for one entirely conjectural battle for the defence of the Stour Line, imagined by Professor Haverfield.

Until Reichsmarschall Goering got to work in the St. George's Street neighbourhood in 1942 it had been a hard task to assemble facts about Durovernum. Ancient Roman sources give only most meagre information—the name and the position of the city, with the implication, from the addition of 'Cantiacorum' to the former, that it was a tribal capital or headquarters. Tessellated pavements had been found at various times in various places in Canterbury, and walls had been noted running across streets where sewers were dug, but no systematic excavation had ever been carried out. On the south and east it was known that the medieval wall, which still stood, was on the line of its Roman predecessor, because a piece of Roman archway can be seen embedded in it near the Queningate, and old prints show undoubted Roman work—since removed—at Ridingate and Worthgate. Cemeteries of cremated remains had been accidentally discovered in Wincheap Green, at St. Dunstan's, near the cavalry barracks in Northgate, at St. Martin's Hill, and near the Old Dover Road at Oaten Hill. In other words, each main route out of Durovernum had a cemetery alongside it, in the usual Roman fashion. But of the plan of the Roman city nothing more was known, and the archaeologists who appeared on the scene in 1944, courting criticism because the war was still in progress, were starting with a virtually clean sheet.

It is indeed true that youngsters on leave from the armed forces, and civilians who had done their stint of part-time service as well as their presumably essential jobs, had abuse shouted at them by members of the patriotic and incidentally stay-at-home British public for digging, in their spare time, in the ruins of Canterbury when they should have been getting on with the war. Their real offence was that of selecting an unusual pastime, in preference to the normal pub-crawling or cinema-sitting, and worst of all, an activity with some intellectual purpose.

But at least they knew what they were doing; this was no aimless prodding around for casual finds, but a properly organised excavation. Some of the diggers were old hands, while others were being introduced for the first time to the fascinating mysteries of archaeological techniques. The modern practitioner works on stratification, and on the basic law that no deposit can be earlier in date than the latest object found in it. He (or she) carefully strips off the layers that have accumulated on the site, one by one, keeping separate the 'dating material'—that is pottery, coins, brooches and other artificial objects from each layer. Coins are best because they date themselves, and even certain types of Roman pottery can be tied down to within twenty years; for brooches and ordinary pots the identifications are not quite so precise. By these stratigraphical methods the excavators can discover when a wall, for example, was built, even though the wall itself gives no clue as to its date. The layer into which the foundations are dug gives a starting date —the wall must be later—and if as usually happens the building has been destroyed and the ground flattened over it, the layers above tell you when this happened, so the life of the wall is known to have extended between these two date-limits. The job of the modern excavator, though it still retains something of the old treasure-hunt pleasures, is much more akin to detective work, and on Roman or Romano-British sites the supply of clues is usually generous; the Romans were most obliging in strewing every site with an ample number of coins and large quantities of broken pottery.

In Canterbury the conditions for digging were pleasant, particularly as long as the supply of basements lasted. The excavator, appearing in the dewy morning with his tools, pushing perhaps past a flowering buddleia (a plant that the ruins much favoured) and picking his way down steps on which the moss was already growing to the basement of a bombed building, would be encouraged in his task by the haunting notes of Bell Harry sounding the matin. Having marked out the area to be attacked, he would then prise up the remains of the modern cellar floor and often would immediately come upon the green disc of a Roman coin or the sealing-wax red gleam of a piece of Samian pottery, for the Roman level was about six or eight feet down, and the cellar-makers had already removed the less interesting upper levels. Some less fortunate diggers were faced with small cramped sites giving little room for manœuvre or even for the deposit of the excavated soil, and with the ever-present danger of breaking into—horror of horrors—a live drain, or, equally disastrous, rooting up a telephone cable. If any wall was found on such a site it invariably continued provokingly under the adjoining un-damaged building, and it was as difficult to record as it was to interpret the partial discovery.

Those were the days before diggers were pampered by big wages, protective clothing and helmets. The Canterbury volunteers were unpaid so that work could go on only at holiday times, never more than ten weeks in the year and often less. It was fourteen years before the supervisor was able to call off his troops, sit back, and try to assess the results.

There had been a few sensational discoveries, but for the most part there had been hard slogging to establish a mass of tiny facts from which a general picture had to be worked out. It was clearly of the first importance to establish the line of the Roman walls, and in this the dig was completely successful; not only in the east and south but for the rest of the circuit also, the mediaeval walls, standing today for half the distance and traceable by isolated bastions for the remainder, follow the course of the Roman ones. In the Westgate Gardens digging uncovered the remains of a small Roman Gateway—the London Gate through which Watling Street emerged and breasted the hill towards Harbledown; and elsewhere proved the date of the walls to be A.D. 270 to 290—late in the Roman period, because of Durovernum's relatively safe situation in the peaceful south-east, protected even from pirate hit-and-run raids by the forts at Reculver, Richborough and Dover. These fortifications enclosed an area of about 120 acres.

The postern in the Westgate Gardens was no chance discovery; the archaeologists were actually looking for it, to test the street plan that they had already produced, based not only on scientific evidence—there was not enough of that—but on flair, guess-work, and a few assumptions as well. There were, however, some solid facts; the postern itself was one and a length of street with rammed gravel metalling five feet thick, near St. George's, was another.

The Roman street plan was nothing like the modern one. The buildings of Durovernum were widely spaced; it was a Romano-British Letchworth, with its community centre—the forum and basilica—somewhere near the place where the County Hotel now stands. And a very nice community centre it must have been, for practically the whole Roman Empire seems to have been scoured to provide the porphyry and marble with which it was decorated; Egypt, Italy, Greece, Africa and Asia Minor. Baths, too, were a feature of Durovernum, public under St. Margaret's Street, and private near St. George's. The houses were of flint and mortar, with half-timbering above, and they were mostly single-storey, with floors often of mosaic or plain tesserae, brightly painted plaster walls, and tiled roofs. Heating was by charcoal stove, or, if you could afford it, hypocaust, hot air central heating. Regret-ably, it was never possible to uncover the whole ground plan of a Roman building; the nearest to this was the find in Butchery

Lane—substantial parts of a town house lie underneath the mediaeval basements. The Corporation acquired the remains, roofed them over, and made them into a show-piece, supplemented by finds from the excavations.

But a much greater discovery, in fact the biggest surprise of the whole series of excavations, turned up on such an awkward, hemmed-in site that it could not be put on show, but could only be back-filled and built over. There is a long story behind the discovery in Canterbury of the largest theatre, so far as is known, in the whole of Roman Britain. The tale begins in the 1860s, when sewers were being laid in Canterbury. The then City Engineer, a Mr. James Pilbrow, was an enthusiastic antiquarian, and made notes of what he found when the trenches were made in the principal streets. Unfortunately, according to a more eminent archaeologist, the late Dr. Haverfield, Pilbrow's jottings, although submitted to the Society of Antiquaries, and received with some acclaim, were merely 'bald and unintelligent notes' and did not result, as did similar operations in Roman cities on the Continent, in the recovery of the plan of the Roman town. But Pilbrow did relate how in St. Margaret's Street, and again in Watling Street, he encountered a concrete structure of such massive dimensions and unyielding substance that after days and nights of assault with every tool available he had to give up the job and burrow under the obstruction. Until the excavations of 1944 to 1957 no one had been able to offer any satisfactory explanation of these massive remains, the only theory being that they formed part of 'the citadel', whatever that was. More than eighty years later the true answer was given and it turned out to be a surprising one. Diggers were sent to explore a small site at No. 3 St. Margaret's Street, which had been unlucky enough to 'get a bomb'. The going was tough. To quote from Professor Sheppard Frere, the Supervisor: 'A maze of walls was revealed but the natural obstacles of the site including live drains, trees and insecure modern foundations of surrounding buildings made their exploration difficult and their interpretation impossible.' To get at the truth, Professor Frere had to go into the cellars of neighbouring properties when he could get at them, which was not always, where more masses of masonry were found; masonry so hard that the cellar builders had given up its removal as a bad job. Plotting all the results on a map, and linking them to Mr. Pilbrow's eighty-year-old data, it was found that the remains represented a colossal D shaped structure, with an outer wall twelve feet and an inner one eight feet thick, and with a diameter of not less than 232 feet. What could it be? Professor Frere had no difficulty in giving the answer—a Roman Theatre, the largest ever to be recorded in Britain. By a supreme feat of archaeological wizardry he was able to date its construction to the years A.D. 210–220, and its final destruction to the years just after the Norman Conquest, and to establish that the building was preceded by another and even wider one, 329 feet approximately in diameter, possibly an amphitheatre.

All in all, the excavations opened the eyes of the archaeological world. No one had suspected that the little-esteemed Roman city of Durovernum would show such signs of opulence, of full-blooded adoption of the Roman way of life, and of continuous prosperity to the bitter end of the Romano-British period. But Canterbury seems always to have a surprise up its sleeve, as future chapters may show.

In the course of ten years digging a vast collection of pottery, coins and other finds was amassed, but the archaeologists never had any luck to compare with the discovery of the silver spoons in 1962 by workmen engaged on constructing Rheims Way, the new inner ring road. In August of that year a local dealer showed the Curator of the Museum an object that had been brought into his shop. It was a spoon, with the handle bent back to make it S-shaped, rather in the style of the spoons made today for those of tender years. It was quickly identified as Roman silver, and gradually the story came out that a number of similar objects, not to mention various ingots, coins and jewellery, had been found by workmen, and were possessed by sundry persons, presumably in ignorance of their value. The missing items were traced and submitted by H.M. Coroner to a somewhat packed jury of local archaeologists, who dutifully condemned them as treasure trove and the property of Her Majesty. As usual, the authorities offered them first to the British Museum on condition that they paid the finders the value of the treasure. The British Museum, after dithering for some time, told the Canterbury Corporation that if they agreed to make the payment they could have the spoons for their own museum. And there they can be seen today. There are:

Two silver ingots
Eleven silver spoons

One silver implement
One gold ring
One hook and eye, gold
One silver pin with green glass head
Eight coins (although there is no evidence that the coins were part
of the hoard)

   An impressive list by all accounts; but what excited the experts
most was the inference that the owner was a Christian. One of
the spoons has, inscribed in the bowl, the chi-rho monogram, a
combination of the first two Greek letters of Christ's name which
was adopted as a Christian badge, and the object described as a
silver implement (it looks like either some kind of winkle-picker
or perhaps a ceremonial button-hook) has the same monogram.
Another of the spoons is inscribed with a name 'Viribonism'
and two lightly scratched figures IV and XII. The ingots may
have been the raw material of a silversmith, melted-down silver
coins from imperial taxes, or, what is thought to be most likely,
a form of hand-out or donative for troops on an emperor's
accession. When things are getting out of hand, whether in
400 or 1973, the men whose lack of co-operation would be
dangerous to the State or its economy have to be kept happy by
sweeteners.

   No period of our history is shrouded in greater obscurity than
that when Britain ceased to be Roman. At the end of the fourth
century we see a Roman province; at the beginning of the fifth,
the protection of the legion's is being taken away by the
emperor; after that nothing is certain until large slices of the
former province are swarming with an immigrant population of
Angles, Saxons and Jutes. How did this come about? Were the
Romano-British inhabitants exterminated? Or did they retreat
into the fastnesses of Wales, Cornwall and Scotland? Did they in
any way mix with the newcomers? In the towns, such as
Durovernum, was there a gap between its abandonment by the
Romano-Britons and its occupation by the Saxons? Until quite
recently, the 'gap' theory was stoutly and pretty generally upheld.
It was said that the Saxons refused at first to dwell in the former
Roman 'chesters' for fear of hobgoblins, or of being infected by
the softness and weakness of those who dwell within city walls;
but the evidence, if any, was purely negative. The bombing of
Canterbury therefore gave a unique chance to test these theories.
What answer did the excavators give? Not a conclusive one—

that would perhaps be too much to expect—but one offering some highly significant pointers.

It is certain that at least one house on the site of what is at present the Marlowe car park, at the rear of the theatre, was occupied by Romano-Britons until the year 428, because coins of that year were found among the ruins. We also know that pieces of pottery, dated from about A.D. 400 and emanating from the Frisian Islands, which were not in the Roman Empire, were left lying about in Durovernum; therefore, while the Romano-Britons were still living in their houses in the city, somewhere in the neighbourhood there were people from the Frisian Islands. It is improbable that Roman provincials would import these crude pots for their own use, and the Roman practice of bringing in barbarian axuiliaries to help fight against other barbarians is a much likelier explanation of them. Even if we are not completely convinced by this evidence there is con-crete proof, in the form of primitive hut-remains, that by 450 Saxons (we use this term to include all members of the invading nations) were ensconced in the former Roman city, their crude shacks being built in alignment with its streets.

Not all of the invaders seem to have had their own womenfolk with them; in the debris of their huts are found the trinkets that Romano-British women loved. These girls may have submitted to the cruel usages of war, but it is pleasanter to hope that the manly beauty of our ancestors would make them willing brides.

The experts are putting the final polish on their report of the excavations, but there is no secret about what they found. It is safe enough to say that, here in Canterbury, if anywhere, there was continuity between the Romano-British and the Saxon periods of our history, and that however crude the manners, however tenuous the thread, some form of civic life may well have spanned the change. Thus the record of Canterbury is germinal to the history of civilisation in our land, and this germinal character of Canterbury's annals must deeply colour its portrait. We must all feel awe and respect for a city which by A.D. 500 was proving itself not altogether unworthy of the boast implied by its Victorian motto: 'Ave Mater Angliae'—Hail, Mother of England.

TWO

BEDE

THE effect of climate on human behaviour is an interesting study. The weather in Canterbury is, on the whole, brighter than in most English cities and towns, and when it is sunny people who earn their living sitting at a desk look round for excuses to get out and about; executives who are not completely dedicated to Mammon rack their brains to think of something in the pleasanter parts that ought to be inspected; bank managers take their time strolling round to the coffee-shop where there are important customers to cultivate. And, many centuries ago, Bertha, the Queen of Kent, could doubtless be heard saying: 'Come, chaplain Luidhard, we must walk to St. Martin's and say a prayer!'

So too the student of Canterbury's past, when all the beauty of the city awaits, will not wish to spend too much time poring over flint axes or silver spoons in the museum. Better to start in the open air and see the ancient stones under the summer sun that has bathed them for centuries, and ponder their meaning on some seat beneath the trees where he can scent the summer flowers and feel the gentle breezes that have crossed the fields of Kent. What finer plan could there be than to follow in Queen Bertha's footsteps to St. Martin's, the focal point of the next stage in Canterbury's story, and the humble and mysterious centre-piece of one of the greatest passages in the history of our island, the return of Christianity?

St. Martin's is humble because it is a tiny church, primitive and with little embellishment; and mysterious because we still do not know by how many centuries it is older than any rival, while its architecture remains ever a puzzling and exciting enigma.

It is quite a step from the museum in the High Street to the oldest church in England, and there are plenty of interesting things along the route which starts at the Buttermarket. But first the High Street, glanced at already, is worth another look.

Mercery Lane with a glimpse of cathedral towers

It is the huge, ugly, four-storey stucco-fronted block, that was built after the great fire in Victorian times (which destroyed most of The Chequer of the Hope, the pilgrims' hostel at the corner of Mercery Lane), that gives the street its misleadingly depressing tone, overpowering at first sight the worthy display of architectures of various old vintages on the opposite side, between White Horse Lane and the St. Mary Bredman rest garden. Prominent is the well-known building containing 'Queen Elizabeth's Guest Chamber'. This has some magnificent pargeting, brightly coloured moulded reliefs showing wreaths of foliage, vines, cherubs or *putti*, and heraldic emblems. So fresh-looking is this decoration that one might suspect a recent 'improvement' to the building, but a watercolour by the Canterbury R.A., Sydney Cooper, painted early in the nineteenth century, seems to show the pargeting as it now is. The name refers to a tradition that when this house was a small inn, Queen Elizabeth I entertained the Duc d'Alençon there. This does not sound, to be quite candid, a particularly likely thing to have happened and there is so far as is known, no documentary proof of, nor indeed basis for, the tale; it is a typical Canterbury mystery, waiting for someone with time to unravel it.

Behind the rest garden is Canterbury's Trevi Fountain. It took considerable skill to keep any semblance of privacy and enclosure in the garden when the building at its rear was converted into a very up-and-coming G-plan furniture emporium, but the shop owners and their architect did the city proud. The rather beautiful wrought iron grille is an excellent visual compromise between the claims of amenity and commerce, screening without hiding the not unpleasing design of the shop, in front of which is the ornamental pool where the public for some reason throw their coins. They must surely be visitors who have learnt the habit in that intimate little square just off the Via del Corso. If so, Canterbury, for once, has followed the lead of another city.

The name, Jewry Lane, of a little street behind the nearby County Hotel is one of the few reminders of the small but wealthy community that lived here until Edward III expelled all Jews from England. When contributions were being levied to meet the ransom of Richard I, Canterbury's Jews paid the third largest amount (exceeded only by their co-religionists of London and Lincoln) so they were presumably the third wealthiest colony in England. Whether Edward III's action should be approved or

B

The old Sun Inn mentioned in David Copperfield
Ridingate roundabout with part of the old city wall

not depends on how strongly one objects to everyone in the town being up to their ears in debt. So far as can be judged, even the wealthiest (such as Terric the Goldsmith and the monks of Christchurch themselves) were well in the red in their dealings with gentlemen with names like Isaac, Jacob and Lazarus. When King Edward so heartlessly anticipated the tactics of certain African politicians there were soon thirteen houses on the market, vacated by members of the departed community.

When Jews were once more admitted, again a community formed in Canterbury, and again the courts were kept busy enforcing notes of hand given by the all-too-improvident citizens to these expert financiers. But one looks in vain for any of them nowadays, and their synagogue has been taken over as a Christian parish hall.

The little show-street of Mercery Lane leads to the Butter-market, once the site of the Bullstake, where the animals were baited before slaughter to make their meat tender. In the seventeenth century the space was thought to be large enough for a building, which after various vicissitudes ended as a theatre; this was removed, to be succeeded by the open-sided Buttermarket building from which the name derives. When this went, in its turn, the little square became the setting first for the memorial to Christopher Marlowe and then for the city war memorial. For some reason it has now become the occasional haunt of hippies, with their dirty jeans, long hair, and unkempt whiskers, strumming guitars, begging for money and using the war memorial as a back-rest while consuming their refreshments. To speak to them, and perhaps remind them of the meaning of the memorial to men and women who died so that the hippies could be free to wear jeans and whiskers, is merely to court an invitation to 'drop dead' or 'get knotted'; the public does not seem to care and a policeman is a rarity in Canterbury these days. But there is solace for annoyance and frustration at the continental-type *terrasse* in the corner of the square, where in summer the overflow from the Olive Branch tavern is accommodated beneath parasols whose bright colours make a gay foil for the Christ Church Gateway, the Dickensian bow-fronted little hotel next to it, and the ancient half-timbered building on Burgate corner. Satisfied with their own wit and virility, the hippies will now perhaps shamble off to annoy the 'squares' somewhere else leaving behind the sharp reminder that before the return of Christianity came the Dark Ages.

The only certain thing about the Dark Ages is that they were very dark indeed. Every history teacher can tell his class the tale of Vortigern and the bad deal he got from Hengist and Horsa and their friends, but every schoolboy understands clearly that although the story provides a useful stock of names for ships engaged in the car ferry service to the Continent, beyond that it is probably a complete myth. Historians and archaeologists have of course investigated the subject, the former handicapped by dearth of material, and the latter by the limitations of their own methods; their technique is excellent for showing in what order events happen, but when, as in the Dark Ages, there seems to be no baseline from which to start, all the pottery, post-holes, occupation-levels, cemeteries and grave-goods fail to supply a solid and dependable story. In Canterbury, between the building of Saxon huts in the centre of the city in about 450 and the events that centre round St. Martin's church in the year 597, there seems to be only a blank, so in going to the church the student, while enjoying the walk, is also being thoroughly scientific; it happens to provide the next piece of solid evidence.

Going eastwards, the first length of Burgate has shops that David Copperfield might well have patronised on his way to school in the Precincts, though the present-day men's fashions, electric drills, package tours, and fancy shop-fitting would have baffled him. From Butchery Lane to Canterbury Lane, Burgate marks approximately the edge of the old blitzed area, and exhibits contrasting philosophies in reconstruction; the buildings on the right show the result when civic planners go into action; those on the left the efforts of the Dean and Chapter, who managed to keep their lands out of the clutches of the planning authority and, with dollars sent by sympathetic Canadians to supplement the regulation war-damage payments, were able to put up nice expensive buildings.

The unsubsidised commercial developers, leasing their plots from the city, and with little money to spare for fancy trimmings, were encouraged to try (with it is hoped at least some success) to build in the idiom of the present but still in a style compatible with a medieval city. By contrast, the Dean and Chapter's Burgate House is neo-Georgian, in a style described as 'highly personalised', 'Baroque', and 'in ghastly good taste'; yet it is warmly praised by almost every lay visitor seeing it for the first time. Is there some lesson in this contrast of outlooks between

Town and Cassock? Medieval architects always built in the style
of their own time, and never imitated that of previous centuries,
so that the City Fathers were both more modern and more
medieval than the Dean and Chapter. Does the study of theology
make the human mind timid, conservative and backward-
looking, or was Burgate House an inspired attempt to play to the
gallery?

The sixteenth-century tower of the demolished church of St.
Mary Magdalen was too solid and incombustible to succumb to
anything but a direct hit, and its genuine antiquity amid so
much that is new emphasises the time-scale of Canterbury.
The war-damage peters out, and the eastern end of Burgate is
back again in the eighteenth, sixteenth and even earlier centuries;
as well as accommodating the architect and the dentist, the
engraver and the photographer, the tobacconist and the florist,
the well-mannered buildings breathe a spirit of calmness, sanity
and peacefulness.

At the end of Burgate where it joins Broad Street a jagged end
of the City Wall, through which it there passes, mutely demands
an explanation. In fact, here stood the medieval Burgate—from
which the street is named—until the last remains of it were removed in 1822. For many years the thoroughfare was officially
named 'Burgate Street', but people had always called it 'Burgate',
and eventually the official practice was brought into line with
popular usage; at the same time the superfluous word 'Street' was
removed from the names of Longport, Wincheap and Northgate.
In the last, the name that was once that of an actual gate applies to
the district as well as the street; Wincheap, too, means the
suburb, as well as the road leading in the Ashford direction.

So the jagged stones edge the gap made when the old Burgate
went. Why then was the wall left in what some would think to
be an unsightly state? The answer is that when Burgate disappeared the broken end was quickly masked by buildings,
including the famous 'Saracen's Head Inn', and so remained until
two or three years ago, when, with much shaking of heads and
genuine reluctance, the City Council removed the buildings to
widen Lower Bridge Street (which continues Broad Street south-
ward). Many people protested loudly—and rightly—at the
removal of a well-known landmark, but there were old buildings
on both sides of the road, and no one could show how to get rid
of the notorious bottleneck of Lower Bridge Street without loss

of some of them. It was the old problem of eggs and omelets.

It is not the policy these days to doctor ancient monuments, so the broken end was simply buttressed and made good against further erosion.

Across Broad Street with its heavy traffic is the vignette of Church Street St. Paul's; the old pub on the left, the church on the right, and the little vista closed by a turreted arch, the old Cemetery Gateway of St. Augustine's Abbey. On the corner of the street housewives with their shopping-bags chatter, while girls in bright-coloured slacks with shoulder-bags make a pleasing contrast with overmuch antiquity; perhaps necessary, when the restaurant on the corner boasts in the lettering painted on its fascia of dating from the *eleventh* century. It certainly has the mediaeval characteristics, upper storey oversailing and leaning slightly outward, windows not quite lined up, roof of weathered tiles; perhaps some relic in the cellars justifies the claim.

The road now jinks to right and then to left, a tangible reminder of the ambitious policies of the old monks of St. Augustine's. Properly, their domain ceased at the high road which in those days continued straight, but, good business men that they were, expert also, it must be admitted, in all manner of forgery and overreaching of the laity, they easily contrived to enlarge their precinct and divert the road at the same time.

On the corner is Sir Edward Hales's eighteenth-century iron water conduit. The little bronze plaque on the nearby house commemorates in Latin and in English the good Baronet's public-spirited act in supplying the conduit at his own expense. Water in Canterbury was a scarce commodity—pure water, that is. Even at the turn of the eighteenth century, Cyprian Bunce the archivist suggested in vain that a little work with a drill in the chalk hills might provide a pure supply such as neighbouring towns enjoyed, but Canterbury preferred to temporise with these iron conduits harnessing the inadequate resources of the local springs.

In Longport the high wall on the left, a mixture of stone, flint and brick, subtly conveys the impression of having been there for centuries; from here, the craftily enlarged precinct of the abbey extended through to North Holmes; from the Cemetery Gate it ran in the other dimension to the lane in front of St. Martin's church. The eighteenth-century building of the old Kent and Canterbury Hospital, ugly and unattractive in its much-altered and much-stuccoed state, has just been removed, and for the first time for 200 years people walking in Longport can see the ruins of the Benedictine monastery and its few remaining buildings, notably the two gateways and the refectory and the Victorian-built St. Augustine's College of which they form part, and can have a better view of the new and not-unattractive teacher training college. The sessions house and prison, further east in Longport, are still within the old monastic boundary. The old court house has a modern extension, and after 170 years the gaol is still in full, or overfull, use; one business at least is flourishing—crime and punishment. The judges and recorders of the Crown Court waiting wearily for the return of the jury with their verdict can look across to the mansion house of the manor of Longport, now a school. It too has additions, and the new assembly hall is canti-levered out over the margin of a still and reedy pool which once supplied water to the city.

There is only one more thing worth looking at before St. Martin's; the group of almshouses on the right endowed by John and Ann Smith, in gratitude for the birth of a son in 1644 after twenty years of childless marriage. They have a mellow charm to which the row of tall chimney stacks, somewhat reminiscent of a pre-1914 naval cruiser, adds a touch of the bizarre.

We are nearly at St. Martin's; on the left is North Holmes Road, flanked by another wall, the featureless high one of the prison. At the end the road turns and a lychgate bowered in trees leads to the oldest church in England. An ancient flint and stone wall retains a rising grassy knoll on which, half shielded by yew and poplar, is a modest square tower with the simplest crenel-lation, a white flag-staff, and a tiny weathercock on a low pyramid of red tiles. Through the lychgate a rather lovely three-pannelled board with the moulded arms of the diocese of Canter-bury surmounting it carries the following message: 'This ancient church is reputed to be the oldest still standing in Europe in which Christian worship has been offered without a break. The Roman brickwork suggests that at one time a Roman temple stood on this site. In the sixth century Queen Bertha worshipped here with her Chaplain, Bishop Luidhard, in the midst of a heathen people; St. Augustine, the first Archbishop of Canterbury, worshipped here with his brethren and began the conversion of the English people. Ethelbert, King of Kent, is reputed to have been baptised in the ancient Saxon font.'

Then from the historical we come to the practical: Sunday services; 8 a.m. communion; 11.15 morning prayer; and so forth. The name of the rector, with his address and telephone number, and those of the verger. Yes, the repute of antiquity may be well-founded, but do not forget this is a real church with a real live rector and verger and congregation, and after nearly fourteen centuries people come here to be christened, like Ethelbert, to be married, and to be buried.

From the noticeboard with its proud announcements the steps lead up to the modest doorway in the western face of the tower between the buttresses and beneath the two little embrasures. A walk round the outside shows that what was said about the use of Roman bricks was no exaggeration. Almost any piece of walling has at least fifty per cent of the unmistakable red tiles worked in with the stone. Further east, the proportion of ancient material increases. Even the nave, which is not the oldest part of the church—that is the chancel—is a building composed mainly of Roman bricks. In the chancel wall, sections of the lower part are entirely so composed. Two ancient arches long blocked up have intrigued, and still baffle, the experts.

The mystery of St. Martin's deepens when one goes inside. The plan is simple—a tower, a nave and a chancel; no aisles, transepts, nor other ecclesiastical trimmings. The ancient walling has been left either completely uncovered, or screened only by loose curtains, so that the bricks, stone, lumps of chalk and flints used by the builders can all be seen, and the result is a conundrum to which perhaps some future Professor Willis—he solved the riddle of the Norman Monastery of Christ Church—may some day give an answer. The general impression given by the inside, as by the outside, is that the first builders were more competent than their various successors who made alterations and additions. Visible in the chancel from the inside are the two arches blocked up by flint and mortar. The jambs are of Roman brick, as neatly laid as in any Roman building, and the rounded heads are of rough, or possibly weathered stones. In the west wall of the nave, well above head level, can be seen three blocked-up windows, the middle one larger than the other two. A good deal of Roman brick has been used even in the process of blocking the windows up. It is clear why the windows had to be filled in—on their outside is the tower, clearly a later addition. The tower, again, has a good deal of Roman brick in its composition.

The suggestion of a Roman temple may or may not be correct, though the idea that Ethelbert was baptised 'in the ancient Saxon font' is quite untenable. What then is the truth? What is the significance of this remarkable building? For an answer we must go to Bede and the historical record.

The Venerable Bede (who died in 735) must have been a delightful character, conscientious and unassuming. He attended all the services in his monastery at Jarrow in case the Second Coming should occur, and Bede be missed from his place by the Almighty; he insisted on the most reliable information before he included it in his history. He tells us that 'in the fourteenth year of the reign of the Emperor Maurice (597) and about 150 years after the coming of the Angles to Britain, Gregory, prompted by divine inspiration sent his servant of God named Augustine and several more god-fearing monks with him, who preached the word of God to the English race.' The sequel is part of English history, although to Kent people, and particularly to Canterbury citizens, there is a special piquancy in the familiar places where it was enacted; the landing with Frankish interpreters near the Wantsum, the message to Ethelbert at Canterbury announcing their arrival and purpose, the reply telling them to stay on the Isle of Thanet until the King of Kent had decided what to do; the presence at Canterbury of Bertha, the Christian queen and her chaplain, Luidhard, the meeting on Thanet resulting in permission for missionary work in the royal city, the first converts. Then in this well-known passage we come to St. Martin's; 'There was nearby on the east of the city a church built in ancient times in honour of St. Martin while the Romans were still in Britain, in which the Queen, who as has been said was a Christian, used to pray. In this church they first began to meet, to chant the psalms, to pray, to say mass, to preach and to baptize until, when the King had been converted to the faith, they received greater liberty to preach everywhere and to build or restore churches.'

One point that Bede does not explain is why St. Martin's church was outside the Roman city and not within its walls as it would be reasonable to expect. The rector's noticeboard suggests there may have been a Roman temple on the site, but that would be no reason, by itself, for building the church there. Although churches were within cities, catacombs and cemeteries were by Roman law required to be outside the city. A Roman cemetery has been found not far from St. Martin's church, alongside the Roman road from Durovernum to Rutupiae or Richborough. This would be a typical situation for a cemetery chapel, or even a large brick-built tomb; therefore a possibility exists that the church was in fact made from the materials of a Roman Christian building connected with burials and cemeteries. One wonders however about the significance of the remarkable fact that the best workmanship to be found in the ancient parts of this church occurs near ground level on the south side, where the coursing of the brickwork is done with expert precision, while the upper and presumably later parts are quite botched and irregular by comparison. This may suggest that St. Augustine brought with him not only missionaries but also technicians, if good bricklayers may be so described, and in fact Augustine reintroduced not only the Roman religion but also some of the other facets of Roman civilisation into heathen and barbaric Britain.

There is some evidence that after a time some of St. Augustine's teaching, especially that about monastic discipline, tended to be forgotten. Have we indications here, in the fabric of St. Martin's, of the same tendency towards gradual degeneration in the useful arts that he and his fellow missionaries introduced, so that while the whole of what St. Augustine taught was not immediately forgotten, the memory faded as time went on?

Once King Ethelbert had been converted, the foundation of the mighty Canterbury Cathedral and the once-mighty St. Augustine's Abbey, and the establishment of the Archbishopric, soon followed, but it was at St. Martin's that it all began, and that is the truth of it. And you can still see the rector's telephone number, and ring him up if you want to!

What Bede says about the foundation of the cathedral is this: 'After Augustine had received his episcopal See in the Royal City he, with the help of the King, restored the church in it which, as he had been informed, had been built in ancient times by the hands of Roman believers; he dedicated it in the name of the Holy Saviour our Lord and God Jesus Christ, and there he established a dwelling for himself and all his successors.'

The last remains of the church that Augustine took over, Lanfranc swept away when he rebuilt in 1070, and the same archbishop ceased to take a daily interest in the life of the monastery, so that it was no longer true to say that it was a dwelling for him. But the dedication of the church to Christ is still unchanged, and there is no doubt that Bede's words describe the foundation of Canterbury Cathedral.

For Augustine's next action the place is given, which brings the events described by Bede all the more vividly to our imagination.

'He also founded,' says Bede, 'a monastery not far from the City to the east in which Ethelbert, encouraged by him, built from its foundations the church of SS. Peter and Paul and endowed it with various gifts so that the bodies of Augustine himself and all the bishops of Canterbury and the Kings of Kent might be placed in it.'

St. Augustine had now got himself well established, and the Pope sent further learned and pious men to reinforce his ministry; also books and manuscripts and, most important of all, the archiepiscopal pallium, or mantle.

As we take leave of old Bede for the time being, we notice that he has said nothing yet of the story of how Pope Gregory, in the market place at Rome, saw fair-haired slave boys and made his famous pun, 'Not Angles but Angels.' Chronologically it comes before Augustine's journey to Britain, yet Bede does not mention it until he is relating the death of the Blessed Pope Gregory when the incident is retailed as what he calls 'a tradition of our forefathers.' The careful Bede does not therefore include it in his narrative of the events but only as an interesting afterthought in his obituary of Gregory.

In Broad Street, northward from where Burgate once stood, is one of the finest remaining stretches of the city wall, with two magnificent round bastions built by Prior Sellinge, and a solid square tower, the work of Prior Chillenden after the monks had agreed to take over the responsibility for keeping this section of the walls in repair. A few feet to the south of Chillenden's tower, embedded in the wall, are some thin red bricks forming part of an arch long ago built up. These are the springing of the arch of one of the Roman gates of Durovernum. A few hundred yards away on the other side of the bastion is a little opening called Queningate, 'The Queen's Gate', and it was through a doorway near here, according to tradition, that Queen Bertha made her way when she was going to St. Martin's for her devotions.

A bare hundred yards to the east, just as Bede describes it, some part of the monastery that St. Augustine founded still stands. Lady Wootton's Green, a short street with two roadways and a pleasant garden between, leads like a little processional way from near the Queningate to the richly ornamented Fyndon Gate, built early in the fourteenth century and now serving to exclude the public, for most of the time at least, from the studious purlieus of St. Augustine's College. With the refectory, which claims the distinction of being the oldest such hall still in use in Europe, the gateway is about the only part of the monastery surviving reasonably intact; both were preserved at the Dissolution through being reserved for royal use. Between 1900 and 1932, the ruins into which the rest of the monastery had degenerated were completely and thoroughly excavated by various people, some of whom were among the country's most gifted archaeologists, and the results are treated by scholars with great awe and respect. They established the fact that for the first few centuries the monastery was a haphazard collection of buildings within one boundary wall, and that there were not one but several churches; not at all what anyone would expect if they were thinking of the efficiently designed, standardised monasteries of the later medieval period. It was almost 400 years before Dunstan reformed, partly rebuilt, and rededicated to St. Augustine, the monastery that the latter founded. Enormous foundations of a circular structure showed that before his death the Saxon Abbot Wulfric had already started work on the famous rotunda that he proposed to erect after Continental models; it was never completed. Most of the Norman and later work went to make cheap building and paving material, which people were allowed to have 'on giving a trifle to the custodian'. Full advantage was taken of this excellent facility. Foundations, bases of pillars and a certain amount of walling remain to show the church plan. Some of the Saxon tombs and foundations, excavated at a lower level, have been kept open and roofed over. Most interesting of all are the ruins of St. Pancras's church which dates back to the time of St. Augustine, an impressive amount of the original walling still remaining. At its zenith in the Middle Ages, St. Augustine's was one of the richest and most influential religious houses in the land, but this happy state was not achieved without some setbacks. When Kent ceased to be a kingdom the royal burials ceased too; and then St. Cuthbert, the eleventh Archbishop, took a hand and obtained the Pope's permission to switch the burial of the archbishops from St. Augustine's to the cathedral, and whether he intended it or not, his own was, by a subterfuge of the cathedral monks, the first body to be interred there.

In the 1940s and 1950s veterans of the National Fire Service would tell of how they saved Canterbury from complete destruction in 1942. How many of them knew that their feat had been anticipated, single-handed, by Archbishop Melitus in the seventh century? We are back again with Bede; he tells us, 'the City of Canterbury had been carelessly set on fire and was rapidly being consumed by the growing blaze which could not be quenched by water. No small part of the city had already been destroyed and the fire was spreading towards the bishop's house. Melitus ordered them to carry him into the path of the flames. The church of the Four Crowned Martyrs stood where the flames were at their highest and the bishop was carried thence and proceeded to avert by his prayers the peril which had defeated strong men. Immediately the south wind veered round to the north and prevented the flames from destroying those places which were in its path. Then it ceased entirely and there was a calm and the flames sank and died out.'

The memory of great events soon becomes befogged with rumour and embellishment; a change of wind is cited as having helped the 1942 deliverance too, but so far it has not been claimed as a miracle.

The precursor of all who, at one time or another, in later centuries strove to make Canterbury a centre and seat of learning, was the seventh archbishop Theodore of Tarsus. Canterbury would not perhaps have attracted such an able man had not his home diocese been captured by the Arabs, making him a sort of refugee. With his close associate Hadrian, he was sent to Britain by the Pope, and became the first archbishop whom the whole English church consented to obey. With Hadrian as abbot of St. Augustine's, the two learned men attracted a crowd of students into whose minds, says Bede, they daily poured streams of wholesome learning; not only the scriptures, but the liberal arts and the Latin and Greek languages were taught. Some of their students knew Latin and Greek just as well as they knew their native tongue.

What was life like in Saxon Canterbury? Directly, we do not know very much; indirectly we can guess quite a lot. We have learnt a great deal, for instance, about the Canterbury of the twelfth century, and it must have been taking shape for generations before the arrival of the Normans. There are one or two instances where new towns seem to have been laid out all at one go during the mediaeval period—the trek from Old Sarum to New Sarum was presumably one of these—but they are pretty rare and Canterbury was certainly not one of them. By the usual method of scrutinising legal documents with lynx-like eyes, scholars are able to tell us that in the seventh century Burgate— the street and its continuation outside the walls—already existed; Ruttington Lane, from its name, is of Saxon origin, and it is pretty certain that the present main street was taking shape. From the exploit of Melitus we know of the church of the Crowned Martyrs, although we are not quite certain where it was, and there was another church dedicated to St. John the Baptist some- where near the cathedral, in addition to St. Martin's, St. Pancras's and the two great monasteries. Another curious fact derived from legal documents is the existence of the right of 'eavesdrip', which gives a picture of buildings crowded together in the centre of Canterbury so that one man's eaves caused another's drips; and there are casual references to the names of a few royal prefects, or praepositi, of the city.

The excavations after the last war produced several hut-sites of the very earliest Saxon period, but very little later evidence. A cobbled yard of the time of Alfred the Great was almost welcomed as proof that the city was not altogether abandoned. Documents show the rather jolly-sounding chapmangild, corresponding approximately to the modern Chamber of Trade, as flourishing; while envied for the money they handled—plenty of which, men were confident, must stick to their fingers—were the moneyers of the King and the Archbishop, for Canterbury was almost as pre-eminent as a supplier of the nation's money as she was in matters spiritual. The city may well, according to officials of the Royal Mint, have had the first mint; certainly by 625 it had one, along with London and perhaps Winchester. By the end of the seventh century the premier mint of the country was at Canterbury, where legal and ecclesiastical coins were struck from a mint in the Monastery of Christ Church. Archbishops and kings not only of Kent but also of Mercia and Wessex issued their coins, but the greatest distinction is to have struck the first penny. Offa, King of Mercia, having reduced the kings of Kent to vassaldom, had them issue from their capital at Canterbury pennies on his behalf and bearing his image. Thus the coin that was to be the basis of the currency for centuries to come, and which even survived the decimalisation of our money, was devised and was first issued at Canterbury. Whether or not it is boastful to claim, as the city's motto does, that Canterbury is the mother of England, it may with complete confidence be asserted that she is the mother of the *Bank* of England.

If we are to believe the Normans when they tell us what they found, there were, in Saxon Canterbury, two very good men's clubs called respectively Christ Church and St. Augustine's, where the gaming stakes were high, and the drinking habits correspondingly low, to the great scandal, one fears of the pilgrims coming to venerate the shrine of St. Dunstan, and the travellers to and from Northern France who would often stop by for the night.

As the excavations produced no trace of Saxon stone buildings, and on the other hand the history books are littered with accounts of the city's being periodically burnt to the ground, either by accidental fires or those started by Danish marauders, it is safe to say that the town was composed of thatched huts.

The people were Jutes, and spoke a dialect of the national tongue, to them melodious, but to us uncouth; sanitation was not their strong point; Danish raiding was endemic, and culminated in the sack of the city and murder of the Archbishop Alphege in 1011. The moneyers, the nobility and the monks probably had a high old time on the whole, but for the common people life was indeed poor, nasty, Jutish and short.

THREE

NEW MANAGEMENT

ALTHOUGH the Norman Conquest was in the long run the making of England, its first and immediate effects were distinctly unpleasant for the native inhabitants.

Your Norman was courageous and energetic, a born leader and administrator, but tough and unsympathetic, regarding religion as a formalised set of rules to be obeyed to the letter rather than in the spirit, and Canterbury was soon to see these characteristics in action.

At the Battle of Hastings the English lords of Kent really did fight to the last man, and were practically exterminated. Any survivors fled overseas, and at least one of them had a distinguished career in the Varangian guard at Constantinople, the medieval equivalent of the French Foreign Legion. After the battle the victors proceeded to march to all parts of England, taking over the government, property and finances of the dead and departed Saxon king and lords, and in the scramble for plunder, Kent and with it Canterbury were grabbed by Bishop Odo of Bayeaux and his underlings. When they heard that the Norman army was approaching after Hastings, the civic leaders had gone out to meet the Conqueror, bowed, scraped, and handed over the keys of the city. William in return had given the hangman the day off and cancelled the order for firebrands. This had staved off disaster for the moment, but Odo's minions, Rannulf de Columbels and Vitalis (a Bayeaux Tapestry character) quickly helped themselves, with the Bishop's approval no doubt, to the lands and houses whose English owners had disappeared. They even went further and seized manors belonging to Christ Church and St. Augustine's, not to mention properties of the City Gild, but once Lanfranc was in the saddle as archbishop he made the adventurers disgorge the church property they had appropriated. The gild, however, had to whistle for its money.

Though his qualification to be regarded as a Norman was based not on his birth, which was Italian, but on long residence in the Duchy, and though he was already sixty-five years old, the new archbishop proceeded to justify the Conqueror's trust by a splendid exhibition of all the best qualities of his adopted country-men. The physical courage that had been shown at Senlac was not required in the cowed and conquered city to which he came in 1070, but he showed great moral courage in taking on the primacy so late in life. In reforming the demoralised chapter of monks at Christ Church and tripling their numbers he demon-strated his qualities of leadership, while the rebuilding of the cathedral and its monastery certainly required, and received, energy and administrative ability of a high order.

The sterner side of the Norman character was shown by the secular administration. It also evinced a spirit of legalism which closely paralleled the formal outlook on religion—a legalism that could justify the invasion of another country on the basis of an oath obtained by a trick, and could incessantly proclaim that it was maintaining the laws of Edward the Confessor while at the same time ensuring that scarcely a single one of Edward's English subjects, or their descendants, was allowed the slightest authority or responsibility in the administration of his realm.

We are told that apart from Westminster the cathedral of Canterbury was the first Norman church to be built in this country, and the present building is still in one sense the cathedral of Lanfranc, added to and altered throughout the ages. After the passage of nine centuries, however, not a great deal remains of his original work; the ground plan of the nave and western transepts is still his, although the actual fabric is from the four-teenth-century rebuilding; some of the walling of the Great Cloister and the Chapter House may be the original vintage Lanfranc, also two or three little pieces in the Infirmary Cloister, if one knows where to look for them, and the ruined arches of the Infirmary itself. But the history of the building is continuous; parts have been renewed, but no one has swept away the whole as did the first Norman primate.

A practice that Lanfranc introduced, and which long persisted, was that of obtaining from Caen the stone for the ashlar work. Some of this material shuttled back and forth across the Channel, being brought here to build St. Augustine's as well as the cathedral, and, when the former had been abandoned, being taken

St. Augustine's College courtyard
The Fyndon Gateway, St. Augustine's College

back to Calais in the time of Mary Tudor to make fortifications. Lanfranc also used tufa, which it is surprising to hear can still be found in mid-Kent, although it is no longer fashionable to use it. Some ecclesiastical historians have accused the archbishop of hasty and shoddy work, because his walls and pillars lasted a mere three hundred years after which some of them began to develop alarming faults and had to be replaced. His ghost might well demur that after three centuries the work was 'out of guarantee'.

By contrast, the church that he built at Harbledown for the leper hospital of St. Nicholas still retains its Norman character- istics; this, with its sister foundation of St. John in Northgate at Canterbury, may well be the oldest almshouse charity in England. Brotherhood Farm, at Hackington, on which a great part of the new university is built, was one of its ancient endowments.

Great as were his achievements at Christ Church, this arch- bishop was, at the same time, the first to regard himself as first and foremost an administrator of the church rather than a monk of the monastery; while retaining the nominal title of abbot, he provided himself with a separate residence and revenues for the maintenance of his primatial office. He probably risked being called, in certain quarters, harsh and unsympathetic, when he used his influence with the Conqueror to secure, in 1072, the Accord of Winchester under which the primacy of Canterbury over York was finally settled. The words are most explicit: 'quod Eboracensis ecclesia Canturiensi debeat subiacere'. One does not know if this document (which is preserved under strict security in the Cathedral Library) was the first *Ebor Handicap*, but it is certainly true as anyone can see that while the other signatories (who include many bishops as well as Lanfranc himself, and, with crosses, King William and Queen Matilda) use the formula *Subscripsi* 'I have subscribed', Thomas of York writes *Concedo* 'I give in'. (Not as an American lady suggested 'I give up'.)

All in all, Lanfranc certainly left his mark on Canterbury.

After him came Anselm, who seems to have been head and shoulders above most other archbishops of Canterbury in sheer in- tellectual power, and the peer of any of them in saintliness of character. Perhaps, coming from Aosta in Italy without Lan- franc's long period of acclimatisation, he did not share the intellectual limitations of a full-blooded Norman. Under him two very able priors, Ernulf and Conrad, refashioned the Choir of the cathedral, building it over a magnificent crypt which is still

Prehistoric mound, the Dane John

extant; dark and gloomy though it may be it is one of the finest showpieces of Norman architecture in this country. The plainness and austerity of the pillars and capitals as devised by Ernulf's and Conrad's masons were relieved a good sixty years later by subtly designed sculpturing of the columns and grotesque and sometimes humorous carving of the capitals—the stones that the pillars support. Later still, in the fourteenth century, the charming little chapel of Our Lady of the Undercroft was inserted into the crypt, so that the sombre work of Ernulf and Conrad forms a dramatic foil to the colour and warmth of the little chapel. But the beautiful Choir of Conrad which the crypt supported was destroyed in the disastrous fire of 1174.

Of the new church that the Norman Abbot Scotland built at St. Augustine's, little remains today, but we can still see prints of the so-called St. Ethelbert's tower, the northwest tower of the Abbey, which lasted until 1822, and is seen to have been a remarkable and rich specimen of the Norman style. (An account of the fall of this structure appeared in the first number of the *Sunday Times* a facsimile of which was recently issued. It was a major artistic loss.)

The harshness and lack of human sympathy of the Normans was evident when they devastated some four and a half acres of the city, sweeping away the little houses to create their castle. The first Normans had made do with a temporary wooden fortress to keep the citizens in order, and this makeshift work may have surmounted the prehistoric earthwork known to this day as the Dane John (a corruption of 'donjon') Mound. In the time of William Rufus, the Conqueror's unpopular son, the permanent castle was built, a sullen and menacing mass of flint and mortar dressed with stones from the ruins of the Roman Theatre. The wreck of the keep still remains, and today gives its name to Castle Street, while mounting guard over the new Rheims Way. But of the curtain walls, towers and surrounding ditch that went with it there is now no trace. Legalism softened in some measure the harshness of the action, and some recompense was made to the displaced owners of the little houses, usually by granting them substitute plots.

The Norman Castle was one of the chain of strongholds built to overawe the English, and the very threat that it represented must have been effective for some time. Later, the forces of rebellion plucked up their courage to attack it, and its record was most inglorious; it never stood a siege, was several times captured, notably by the French Dauphin in 1216 and by Wat Tyler in 1381, always surrendered, and finally was used by the citizens as a gasworks and suffered other indignities until one-third of the fabric and all claim to comeliness and pride had been lost. Eventually, a well-meaning but tardy local authority took on the guardianship of what remained, to the plaudits, no doubt, of the mocking shade of Richard Harris Barham who had written:

> The Keep, I find, 's been sadly altered lately,
> And 'stead of mail-clad knights, of honour jealous,
> In martial panoply so grand and stately,
> Its walls are filled with money-making fellows,
> And stuff'd, unless I'm misinformed greatly,
> With leaden pipes, and coke, and coals, and bellows;
> In short, so great a change has come to pass,
> 'Tis now a manufactory of Gas.

We can add a tailpiece to the sketchy chronicle of the Norman period in Canterbury. The proverbial schoolboy and schoolgirl know that the story of the Norman invasion and the Battle of Hastings is depicted on the Bayeux Tapestry. In an article on the style and design of this well-known work, Professor Wormald remarks, 'Where the work of designing the composition was carried out will never be known. Yet it will be recalled that there was at this time an accomplished school of drawing at Canterbury. By 1067 Odo was already Earl of Kent with his headquarters in the county. If he did order his embroidery in England (and on stylistic grounds, Mr. D. A. Harding thinks that he did) then Canterbury would be a good candidate.

Canterbury is far from destitute of relics of the Saxon period—in nomenclature, in coinage, in at least one church and fragmentary pieces of others, and most of all in the memory of events that moulded its history. But usually the Norman broom swept clean; of the entire Saxon Cathedral and monastery of Christ Church nothing was allowed to remain; at St. Augustine's not even the beginning of Wulfric's famous rotunda. Exceptionally, the little church of St. Pancras in the St. Augustine's precinct was not quite razed to the ground, and we still have some of its Saxon walling at the present day.

At all events the Normans made a new start, and from their time Canterbury's history, civic and architectural as well as ecclesiastical, flows in a continuous stream, so that we are left, not with memories and fragments of walls, but with solid and massive buildings complete and still in use, and as the Norman merged into the Angevin age, the foundations were laid of Canterbury's present civic life and institutions.

It was after the reign (or rather the anarchy) of King Stephen, that the kings of England became not strictly-speaking Normans but Angevins, otherwise Plantagenets; but the style of civilisation and architecture, and the blood of the French occupants of all the other positions of authority in the country, were unchanged; and Canterbury still speaks of them as Norman. Spanning the last few years of King Stephen's reign and the first years of that of his Angevin successor, Henry II, was the priorate at Christ Church of Wibert. Dazzled by the later and perhaps more spectacular works of Thomas Chillenden, critics do not seem to accord to Wibert the place to which he is surely entitled in order of greatness among the priors of Christ Church; some put him after Henry of Eastry and Sellinge, let alone Chillenden. But admirers of Wibert (or Wybert) will not let his claims go by default; he produced two separate masterpieces of architecture that have survived to the present, and, what is more, he installed modern-style plumbing; yes, in the 1160s he put in piped running water and drainage as well. The supply was brought from settling tanks on higher ground far outside the city walls to the famous Water Tower on the north side of the cathedral, and from there was distributed to all parts of the monastery.

The present-day cathedral Treasury, a well-preserved piece of classic Norman architecture of creamy Caen stone, began its life as a monastic building in Wibert's time, and is well known to students of architecture; another of Wibert's famous buildings is the Norman Staircase near the north-west corner of the Green Court; richly arcaded, and roofed over, it is a relic of the New Hall that he built, it is said, to house poor pilgrims.

Not the least interesting aspect of Wibert's waterworks is the manner in which the story became known to us. Many of the volumes, if not from the monastic library then certainly from its scriptorium, have found their way (in circumstances that we prefer not to investigate) into the libraries of various Oxford and Cambridge colleges. In the library of Trinity, Cambridge, is a great psalter which for some reason contains within its covers two remarkable drawings prepared by Wibert and his assistants, the subject of which is the system of water supply and drainage that the prior installed about the year 1164.

Scarcely less astonishing than the discovery that a system of almost modern-type plumbing existed here over eight hundred years ago is the survival of these plans, drawn to scale and very accurate. In the nineteenth century the brilliant architectural historian Professor Willis got to work on Wibert's plans, supplementing his study with careful field work, and as a result was able to recover the entire plan and layout of the monastery as it was in the twelfth century. This was one surprise; another was the discovery that over eight hundred years later, and four hundred years after the Dissolution, there are few of the buildings of which *some* trace cannot be seen above ground today, if no more than a wall, a doorway or a ruined arch. And many others are actually still going strong as complete structures. Once this idea has sunk in, a stroll round the Precincts takes on a new meaning; instead of a casual study of old buildings and picturesque remains it becomes an exciting exercise in reconstructing the past.

Some of the monastic buildings were taken over by the Dean and Chapter for use as adjuncts to the cathedral, and remain substantially intact. This is true, for instance, of the Great Cloister. It is not accidental that the words 'cloister' and 'monk' are so closely associated, because the whole life of the monastery radiated from the cloister; it was the place where the monks lived, when they were not actually eating, sleeping, or attending services. One can even see in the south aisle (that is, the one next to the cathedral) holes and grooves where there was glazing to give some protection from the weather to the blue and shivering brethren in what must have been a very draughty place. Practically every stone here tells its own story, and this cloister has been described as a museum of all the different styles of mediaeval architecture for the edification of students. In its present form (but not in its ground plan, which is much earlier) it dates from the later fourteenth century, and some claim Henry Yevele, the architect of the nave of the cathedral, as the designer, partly on the ground that the cloister was rebuilt at the time that Yevele was in charge of the more important work. An unusual feature is the enormous number of ornamental bosses in the vaulting, including no less than 800 coats of arms, thought to be those of the people who subscribed to the work. Some bosses are ornamented with carvings of human faces, and one of these is put

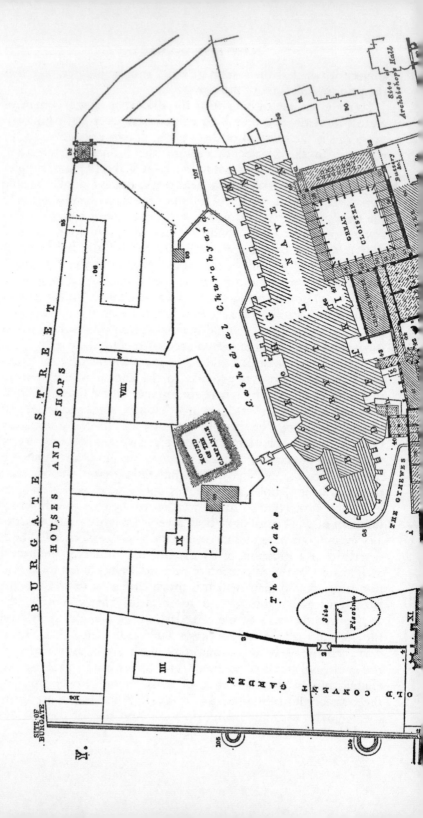

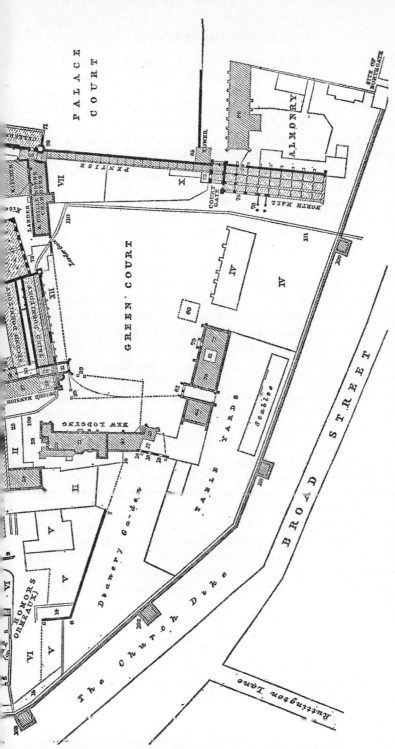

Christ Church, Canterbury: plan of the Priory and Archbishop's Palace (from the plan drawn by Professor R. Willis from his survey 1845–68, and reproduced in the journal of the Kent Archaeological Society).

forward as representing Yevele himself. The doorway in the north-west corner led, in the twelfth century, to the Archbishop's palace and figures in the story of Thomas Becket which forms the subject of the next chapter. At the side of this door is another strange little feature, typical of the queer little objects to be seen in Canterbury that could easily pass unnoticed. It consists of an octagonal opening in the cloister wall, which was probably a surreptitious serving hatch for handing a quiet glass of beer to a thirsty monk.

There is one argument that weighs very heavily against the theory that the reconstructed cloister was designed by Yevele—the work is to some extent botched. Both the fine doorway leading from the cloister into the part of the cathedral known as the Martyrdom, and the trefoil arcading of the north wall of the cloister—originally the outer wall of the monks' refectory—have been badly mutilated by the unsympathetic way in which the later work has been superimposed upon the earlier without any attempt to blend or marry the two together. One can scarcely see the hand of the master in this sorry effort.

Another monastery building still intact is the Chapter House, leading from the cloister on the east; built by Lanfranc, it was reconstructed by Henry of Eastry in the early fourteenth century, and again altered by Thomas Chillenden, so that the lower part of the wall is in the Early English style of Eastry's time with trefoil arcading, and the upper in Perpendicular. To this day the Chapter House plays a useful part in the life of the cathedral and the city; it was here that Eliot's *Murder in the Cathedral* was first performed. The dormitories, and the buttery, refectory, and cellarer's quarters adjoining the cloister, and the kitchens were at the rear of the refectory. Although all these buildings have been destroyed, except for fragmentary remains, the walls separating them from the cloister, and the doorways that led to them from it, are still there to see, and show clearly the layout of the buildings, though now they lead only to the gardens of the dwellings of high ecclesiastics.

Two of the four aisles of the Infirmary Cloister also remain, to form part of the passageway from the Great Cloister to the Green Court; and jutting into the southern aisle of this second cloister is the famous twelfth-century Water Tower, which was also a washing place for the monks on their way to the services in the cathedral. It is an octagonal chamber in the Perpendicular style of Chillenden's priorate with a conical roof, supported on the circular, vaulted substructure that Wibert built. This picturesque relic has been ill cared for, its ancient stones being supported by later buttresses of flint and even red brick; but the vaulting, protected from the weather, is still in good condition. The little building shows what the French mean by the phrase 'château d'eau'.

All the ground between the cathedral and the city wall was within the precincts of the monastery, and many houses, now occupied either by members of the Chapter or by the King's School, were formerly conventual buildings. Most are clustered round a large area of greensward called the Green Court which in fact exactly represents the Great Court of the monastery, an open space provided as a kind of *cordon sanitaire* to separate the secluded quarters of the monks from what were called the menial buildings; the brew houses, granaries and so forth, and stables, where the lay servants of the monastery worked. Also in this area were the buildings devoted to hospitality, whether housing important persons or poor pilgrims. The rambling Deanery to the east of the Green Court was—in much different form, from that in which it has come down to us after the numerous alterations that it has suffered—a building devoted to hospitality for distinguished visitors. The brew houses and stables are now converted to King's School use, as is the Mint Yard, the name of which requires no explanation.

In another peaceful area to the east of the cathedral is the great building known as Meister Omers. This, now a boarding house of the King's School, was once another lodging for important visitors to the Priory. Between it and the cathedral extends the row of Norman arches which are what remains of the Infirmary Hall, with what is left of the Infirmary Chapel to the east.

The dissolution of the monastery resulted in an orgy of destruction, to be followed by centuries of neglect and indifference, yet he who wanders amid the Green Court, the Cloister and the ruins of the Infirmary will reflect that after all that has happened a great part of the Priory of Christ Church still survives in one degree or another of ruin, preservation or modern adaptation, and that with every step the modern tourist looks upon the very stones that were familiar to the monks of old.

It is only proper to conclude this account of the Norman monastery of Christ Church with a word of warning. For nine months in the year the Green Court is the Quadrangle of one of England's great public schools, and the scene of much cheerful activity, but when the school is on holiday complete peace and quiet descend, the only movement being that of the occasional visitor sampling the splendid views of the cathedral to be seen from here, or perhaps a strolling clergyman deep in thought.

But when darkness falls on the Green Court and the alleys and courtyards leading from it, there may be another visitor, from whom the mortals who frequent these purlieus shrink in dread. In the chilling blackness of the Dark Entry, within Prior Sellinge's Gateway, lurks the ghastly phantom of Nell Cook, a spectre that links the terror of the supernatural with the memory of a grave clerical scandal. Our friend Richard Harris Barham calls his account of this macabre affair *The Legend of the Dark Entry—The King's Scholar's Story*. After relating a King's Scholar's terror of going through the Dark Entry at night for fear of Nell Cook, the poet tells in ironical terms how a portly Canon had a house fast by the Entry and—

> Ellen Bean ruled his cuisine. He called her 'Nelly Cook.' . . .
> People said no clerk had need of such a pretty cook.

We then hear that one Whitsun Eve a gay lady, supposedly his niece, arrived to stay at the Canon's house. The jealous Nelly then finds her way into the Oxford Book of Quotations with the line:

> They were a little less than 'kin,' and rather more than 'kind.'

To test her suspicions, she hides the poker and tongs in the gay lady's bed, and after six weeks:

> . . . the poker and the tongs unheeded lay!
> From which, I fear, it's pretty clear that lady rest had none;
> Or, if she slept in any bed, it was not in her own.

Nell then applies her eye to the keyhole of the Canon's bedroom door, and as a result of what she sees, there follows some skulduggery with a doctored pie, after which the Canon goes missing. When he is found—

> The Canon's head lies on the bed—his niece lies on the floor!
> They are as dead as any nail that is in any door!

Soon afterwards, Nell Cook herself disappears from mortal view, but there are heavy hints of a granite stone, fresh mortar and furtive-looking monks. A hundred years later, the stone having worked loose, the Dean's masons discovered a female skeleton beneath it. A doctor examines the bones—

'I should not be surprised' said he, 'if these were Nelly Cook's!'

Of the three masons who found the remains two were later hanged for murdering the third, and—

Whoso in that Entry dark doth feel that fatal breath
He ever dies within the year some dire untimely death!

Hence the King's Scholar's prudent aversion from this deadly place; hence also this timely warning to the unsuspecting reader.

FOUR

ST. THOMAS OF CANTERBURY

I am not in any danger, only near to death.—Eliot

IN painting a portrait the artist must decide which of the characteristics of the sitter shall be brought out, and which shall be toned down. It is not beauty alone that lies in the eyes of the beholder; ugliness, pleasantness, unpleasantness, importance, and unimportance are also subjective impressions. What significance then for the reader of today has the story of the quarrel between Thomas Becket and King Henry II? Everyone knows at least the salient features; Becket's friendship with Henry; the change in him when he became archbishop; the resentment of the King; Henry's final impetuous outburst; the murder by the four knights, and Henry's repentance of his words and humble penance. It would be easy to say that no one either in Canterbury or anywhere else cares any longer about the issues on which Henry and Thomas were disputing; after all, the controversies—about the pre-eminence of Canterbury over York, the right to try 'criminous clerks' and to control the life and conscience of the church—have in fact been settled for centuries. The clash of the royal weapons—fines, banishment, threats of imprisonment or worse—and those of the church—excommunication, suspension, anathema and interdict; the journeyings, confrontations, flights and plottings all seem barren of interest today.

Does anyone, it may be asked, really warm to Becket as a man? Or is he simply a remote historical figure? Is not the real interest of the martyrdom, the pilgrimages and the miracles, their effect on the fortunes of the city and cathedral? This line of reasoning is exactly what the tempter of Thomas whispered in his ear in T. S. Eliot's play *Murder in the Cathedral*:

> When miracles cease and the faithful desert you
> And men shall only do their best to forget you
> And later is worse when men will not hate you

> Enough to defame or to execrate you
> But pondering the qualities that you lacked
> Will only try to find the historical fact.

But somehow, the story of Thomas and Henry, and the riddle of their characters and motives, still appeals to those of deep intellect such as Eliot, and can still inspire works of genius such as his best-known play in which the tempter is given his answer:

> For wherever a saint has dwelt, wherever a martyr has
>   given his blood for the blood of Christ,
> There is holy ground, and the sanctity shall not depart
>   from it,
> Though armies trample over it, though sightseers come
>   with guide books looking over it.

Becket and Henry each had the unhappy knack of bringing out the worst in the other. With a more reasonable archbishop, Henry might have gone down in history as a monarch firm but fair in his dealings with the church; with a less headstrong king, Becket might have had nothing worse to fear than mild irritation at his foibles. Thomas's actions as archbishop were calculated to raise the hackles of a man like Henry, while Henry's implacable resentment must have made Thomas feel that the king's former friendship could only have been skin-deep.

Thomas was also unlucky in having got up the backs of two or three of the leading bishops. If the whole church had presented a united front with Thomas and the Pope, Henry would probably have been outwitted without any violence.

Nevertheless, Becket was responsible for errors of judgment so great as to amount to flaws of character; never giving the King a chance to ponder and possibly reconsider; constantly flying off the handle; acting precipitately and without taking advice; handing out excommunications right, left and centre; marring his undoubtedly courageous character by violent language and demonstrations of personal bitterness, until the impartial judge must say, in handing out blame between king and archbishop for the catastrophe that followed, that it was six of one and half a dozen of the other.

Finally, Thomas was often inconsistent; as after Fréteval when, having made an apparently insincere and half-baked reconciliation with King Henry in Normandy, he returned to England looking for trouble, or a martyr's death, or both, refused to revoke the excommunications of various bishops who had incurred his displeasure, and tried to pester the King's son, the young Henry, with his grievances.

The final dénouement began on Christmas Day, 1170, when Thomas preached in his cathedral telling his flock of his impending martyrdom; and then excommunicated more of his enemies.

It was obvious that things could not be left like this; with the King out of the country there was the constant probability of disaffection and possibility of rebellion. Talk went on in Normandy of silencing Thomas by imprisonment; then in a climax of frustration Henry let fly with his jibe at 'the idle cowards' who allowed him to be mocked so shamefully by 'a low-born clerk'.

It is not thought that the four knights (Hugh de Morville, William de Tracy, Reginald Fitz-Urse and Richard le Breton), who were no mere adventurers but men of substance, set out on their mission with murder in their hearts; perhaps they meant only to imprison Thomas, but were goaded by his defiant taunts and the menaces of a hostile crowd; possibly they had no clear idea how they intended to silence him, and were talked into murder by the archbishop's deadly enemies, the de Brocs of Saltwood Castle. We shall never know what they thought, only what they did.

The date was 29th December. At three o'clock in the afternoon the knights forced their way into the archbishop's hall, unarmed. Their interview with him was quite fruitless, and ended with raised voices: 'You know where you can find me,' Thomas shouted after them. He had refused to discuss things calmly, or to seek the advice of his own council; he could only harp on the fact that he was ready to be martyred.

The knights had left their arms in a certain mulberry tree in the garden outside; arming themselves, they tried to come back into the hall. It was locked, so they started to smash their way in. Thomas was then persuaded by his friends to go—but with exasperating slowness and deliberation—to the cathedral. With armed men all round, the only way was by a little-used door (which can still be seen) in the Great Cloister. It was locked and the bolts were rusty. Where was the key? Who was strong enough to move the fastenings? The knights' shouts were drawing nearer when in the nick of time two hefty servants of the cellarer brought the key and forced back the bolts. The retainers dragged Becket into the cathedral and the monks slammed and locked the door, but he immediately told them to open it again. Still itching to confront the knights, Thomas was seized by the monks and dragged unwillingly to the steps leading to the High Altar; there was nothing to stop him escaping either into the crypt or into the innumerable recesses of the darkened building, but when the knights appeared with drawn swords he broke loose from the monks and faced the intruders. De Morville went through the routine of repeating their demands, and Thomas that of refusing to comply. Then he showed great chivalry in seeking a respite so that his clerks could leave the scene to be safe from the trouble that was clearly coming.

The argument between Thomas and the knights quickly developed into a shouting-match, and the shouting-match into a brawl; Fitz-Urse gripped the archbishop's cloak; with a hurtful epithet Thomas shook him loose and sent him reeling, a dangerous thing to do to an armed man. Murmuring the Norman-French equivalent of 'I'll get you for that', Fitz-Urse came back with cold steel and drew first blood, cutting the top of Thomas's scalp; Tracy struck, and then le Breton gave the *coup-de-grâce* by cutting off the top of the archbishop's head. As Becket crashed to the ground and lay still, the murderers rushed out of the cathedral, yelling war-cries. Silence descended, as the smell of fresh blood mingled with the sharp odour of the incense.

The consequences of Becket's sacrifice—could even he have foreseen them?—were immediate and dramatic.

A cry of horror resounded through Christendom, bringing a wave of emotion comparable to that which followed the assassination in our own time of President Kennedy. King Henry had to bow before the storm, and there was nothing left for him to do but to give in and to go cap in hand to the Pope to make the best terms he could. Alexander III seems to have been a better diplomatist than either Henry or the martyred Becket, and wisely did not extract the last ounce of flesh from his helpless opponent. While these events were in progress miracles—the qualification 'or what were accepted as miracles' is still not agreeable to some— miracles, then, were taking place at Thomas's tomb. Modern books, however, do not give us very much detail about these wonders—the cult is now out of fashion. As illustrated in the windows of Trinity Chapel, they seem usually to have involved the curing of ailments, or rescue from a variety of dangerous situations. For instance, a gentleman from Gloucester, buried alive while laying drainage pipes, is successfully dug out and resuscitated thanks to the intercession of St. Thomas; in another series of pictures a boy, apparently drowned, is brought back to life by the same supernatural assistance.

The saint's wonder-working powers had, however, a less pleasant use, and those who, after benefiting from them, failed to make due financial recognition to the church, soon experienced, in sickness or bereavement, the painful effects of his resentment.

Soon, the fame of the miracles led to pilgrimages, and pilgrimages led to further fame. The pilgrims came not only, as Chaucer relates, from every shire of England, but from all parts of Christendom from Iceland to Antioch. And these pilgrimages were the outward manifestations of an inner spiritual revival, touching not only England but also many Continental countries as well, and comparable to the revival of religion under the Wesleys.

We must not be too censorious about the religious frenzy that surrounded the shrine of Becket. In the twelfth century saints and martyrs were the only figures available to receive the hysterical admiration that now goes to pop-idols.

Although Chaucer speaks with apparent piety about 'the holy blissful martyr', his *Canterbury Tales* are really something of a send-up of the pilgrims, if not of the pilgrimages, of his own day. The martyr, whose fame had attracted Louis VII of France, Richard Coeur-de-Lion and John of England, and William the Lion of Scotland, was scarcely flattered by the visits of Chaucer's pardoner, summoner, and wife of Bath. But it is unlikely that the poet was echoing a general disenchantment as, even a hundred years after his time, the highest in the land continued to venerate the shrine, and it almost seemed as if the issue of the Wars of the Roses hung on the apparently fickle favours of St. Thomas.

Ecclesiastical writers naturally expatiate on the prosperity that the pilgrimages brought to the cathedral and to the city, and even go so far as to contend that the city would be a most obscure place had it not been for the boost then given. They probably exaggerate; Canterbury had been a place of importance long before the days of Becket, and as will later appear, has managed to survive with reasonable success the disappearance of his shrine. The modern sightseers and tourists probably come in even greater numbers than the mediaeval pilgrims; but an important cricket match at the St. Lawrence ground will cause more

Norman staircase near the Green Court

congestion and dislocation than was ever created by the attractions of the cathedral or the fame of Becket.

Five hundred years after Chaucer the story of Becket began to produce its own literary harvest; controversial historical or semi-historical plays by such masters as Alfred Lord Tennyson, Christopher Fry, T. S. Eliot and the Frenchman Anouilh. The last-named made the Norman ascetic Becket into a Saxon woman-chaser, but could justly claim to be following the tradition established by Queen Victoria's Poet Laureate of adopting the literary standard of a troubadour rather than the truthfulness of a historian.

Tennyson introduces into his play *Becket* the Fair Rosamond, mistress of Henry II, and her hidden bower at Woodstock. Becket, we are told, personally rescued Fair Rosamond from assassination by Henry's wife Eleanor of Aquitaine and Reginald Fitz-Urse, and took Rosamond to the nearby nunnery of Godstow. Henry, having heard a garbled account of this transaction from Eleanor, completely misread Thomas's motives (which had been of the purest) and, according to Tennyson's play, it was Henry's jealousy of his mistress that provoked the notorious outburst and Becket's murder. Even more boldly Tennyson invents a new martyrdom story in which Rosamond is present, disguised as a monk. She is held screaming and struggling in the arms of one of the knights while the foul deed is done. Small wonder that this play was Tennyson's biggest theatrical hit!

Why is it that in both Tennyson's and Eliot's plays there is a suggestion that the knights were inflamed by drink? Is there some ancient source, from which both playwrights drew, that warrants this assertion? What is even more puzzling is that when asked for his reasons Eliot denied having given the impression that the knights were drunk, and spoke of misinterpretation by actors. He must have forgotten his own stage direction '. . . the knights enter, *slightly tipsy*' and Tracy's speech at the end, 'I had drunk a good deal . . . If we seemed a bit rowdy, you will understand why it was'. So the mystery remains.

On the more important question of Thomas's character and conduct much has been written by many people. Defoe says bluntly that Becket and others 'plagued, insulted, and tyranniz'd over the kings of England, their soveraigns, in an unsufferable manner', but perhaps the most convincing analysis is that of Professor David Knowles, who avoids going to the other extreme

5

The ancient church of St. Martin
Poor Priests' Hospital

and suggests that Becket, a promising protegé of Archbishop Theobald, had decided to devote his life to the service of God before he accepted from the king the Chancellorship of England. In so accepting Thomas allowed himself to be attracted, by worldly things, from the course that he had set for himself, and thus he lived a divided and fundamentally dissatisfied life; so when later he assumed the archbishopric it was with an even more determined resolve to devote all his efforts to the service of Christ. When the challenge came, he was anxious to plunge in with all the energy that he possessed and prove himself un-dividedly loyal to the church. A modern psychologist would say that because of his guilt complex he overreacted to the situation that was presented to him.

Although formally beatified, because of his death as a martyr, Becket did not otherwise come up to the standards of saintliness. He was in fact a typical Norman, and the typical Norman was no saint. His was not the gentleness, generosity, love, lack of self-seeking, equanimity and self-control that a saint should have. In the strictest sense he was not even a martyr, as he did not die for Christianity, but rather for the rights of the Archbishop of Canterbury, and for church property and jurisdiction. But the heavy price he paid demands that we judge his actions broadly, and with compassion. In that sense he died for the spiritual freedom and authority of the Church, and for that cause he went to his death with his eyes open.

Of all the fires that in ancient times devastated Canterbury and its monuments, the best documented is the one that took place on the 5th September, 1174, and destroyed the eastern part of the cathedral. The origin of the fire is interesting. The wind carried sparks from the burning thatch of cottages in Burgate to the roof of the cathedral, drove them under the joints, and fanned them until they set fire to the rafters (for Conrad's Choir was not stone-vaulted, but had a wooden roof). So often has this tale been repeated that it is pleasurable to hear some new facet of the story. Dr. William Urry suggests that Lambin Frese, the moneyer, may have played a part unintentionally in this episode. Before the fire Lambin had a workshop in front of Christ Church Gate, but within three years of that calamity he moved to a new site in Stour Street, far from the cathedral, and the monks showered him with money and legal help to hasten his departure. May it not have been sparks from Frese's furnace that set fire to the workshop and then to the cathedral? However that may be, the monks, possibly helped by the citizens, were unable to control the flames. They hurriedly removed the most valuable things, or what in their eyes were the most valuable—saintly relics and so forth—in the nick of time, just before the roof collapsed on to the wooden furniture below, causing such an inferno that the Choir was irreparably ruined.

Prostrated with grief, the monks could not help wondering at the inscrutable dispensations of the Almighty. After holding a kind of selection board or short list of aspirants for the commission, they sought architectural advice about reconstruction from Guillaume de Sens, who had to be very circumspect in imparting his conviction that apart from the external walls everything must be taken down and built afresh, as the flames had made the pillars quite unsafe. Eventually the brethren had to face the unpalatable truth; and once they had got used to it they realised that they had a glorious opportunity to plan the rebuilding magnificently, to form a worthy setting for a shrine of Thomas of Canterbury, Saint and Martyr, whose fame was already spreading through Christendom.

Their enthusiasm mounted; the new choir must be larger and more stately than the old. 'Spare no expense, Master Prior,' they urged; 'we have all the time in the world; if the cash runs out this year, close the job down until the coffers are full once more, next year or the year after, for that matter.'

Everything must be of the best: workmanship, artistry, materials; the new choir was to be the first building in England in the brand-new Gothic style, with pointed instead of rounded arches, and pillars of black marble would contrast with the creamy white of the stone columns. Nothing was too good for the martyr. More than this, its whole form was to be quite unusual; the place intended for Becket's shrine would be raised up over a lofty crypt so as to convert this part of the cathedral into an awe-inspiring setting, like the approach to a throne room. It was as if the monks and their architect could already see centuries into the future when, basking in the glory of Thomas's reputation, shrine and relics, the cathedral would become and remain the goal of pilgrims from every part of Christendom.

The rebuilding was not, alas, without incident. Of the two gifted architects who successively directed this great enterprise,

Guillaume de Sens had the ill luck to fall off the scaffolding and receive serious and incapacitating injuries. He struggled gamely to carry on from his sick-bed, but in the end had to retire defeated to his native France. Fortunately his assistant, William the Englishman, was on hand to take his place, using the plans that Guillaume had prepared, but improving, if possible, with lighter and more graceful work, on the execution.

As one can see today, the floor level of the body of the Choir is already well above that of the Nave, and further ranges of steps raise Trinity Chapel above the level of the Choir; a majestic and original conception.

By using the walls of Anselm, and retaining the two towers which abutted on the curve of the apse, the new builders obliged themselves to narrow the width of the new Choir, but beyond the two towers the new building could burst through the walls of the old to form a new Trinity Chapel and ambulatory, with the round chapel or corona beyond to the east; and the width of the new extension could gradually increase before it closed in again with the new apse. Although it is common ground that this eastern extension of the cathedral was designed as a resting place for the body of Becket, yet the monks delayed this consummation for many years; until the year 1220 in fact, when the body was 'translated' from its place in the crypt to the new shrine in Trinity Chapel with such well-announced pomp that the King himself, Henry III, the Archbishop of Rheims, and the Papal Legate, headed the great company supporting Archbishop Stephen Langton and a host of bishops and abbots at the stately ceremonies, and with such disregard of money considerations that by the time the archbishops had finished paying the bills, the jubilee of the 'translation' was upon them.

Although the shrine was removed on the orders of Henry VIII at the Reformation, its site is clearly to be seen, and modern visitors can discern the exact line, marked by a groove in the tiled floor, to which mediaeval pilgrims were allowed to proceed when venerating the shrine to the east. Keen-eyed antiquarians have also discovered what they consider to be traces in the broken pavement of the iron rail that surrounded it.

The crypt that William the Englishman built to support the chapel is far and away the largest and finest in England. One fact tells more about it than either statistics or superlatives can; all through the last war it was used, without loss of dignity or notable inconvenience, for the normal services of the cathedral. On this lower level, too, one can see exactly where the 'glorious choir' of Conrad terminated. The Norman work stops on the curved line of the former apse, beyond which there is a transformation to a new world of light and spacious dignity. Canterbury, faithful to the memory of her patron saint, bears as part of her own the arms assigned to him; three Cornish choughs, but the Trinity Chapel—harbinger as it was of the new style of architecture that was destined to reach superb heights of daring and magnificence—created as the setting for the martyr's shrine, is the most impressive and tangible relic at the present time of the sacrifice of Thomas of Canterbury.

FIVE

BLOWING THEIR OWN TRUMPET

CANTERBURY still has its Burghmote Horn, and uses it on high ceremonial occasions. The city fathers have never quite got used to the idea that since the Reform Act the medieval Burghmote no longer exists, and when they address the city council they are still apt to use the expression 'this court', just as their predecessors had done since before the time of Becket.

When he was chancellor, Thomas witnessed the charter that Henry II granted to the city round about the year 1155, in which the 'Burgihmot' is spoken of as an institution already working. What else do we know about the city in the first century after the Norman Conquest? There are a few bald and cryptic references in the Domesday survey, and the solid fact of the building of the castle. A scene may be imagined of roystering churls, clanking men-at-arms, and busy merchants, and from the uphill work of gathering isolated facts and making deductions from them some glimmering of the truth may emerge, but the scene in general is shrouded in obscurity.

Then suddenly, in the year 1166, all is changed; one minute we are groping in the dark, and the next moment we are blinded by the light—not just a ray here and a shaft there, but a flooding of the whole with noonday brilliance. This almost theatrical transformation is the result of Dr. William Urry's work on the rentals of the monks of Christ Church. Dr. Urry has been able to prepare plans of the Canterbury of 1166, and of the Canterbury of 1200, showing not only streets, churches and other public buildings, but the very plots on which named tenants had their houses, shops, workshops and gardens. He has also transcribed and printed the rentals themselves in *Canterbury under the Angevin Kings*. To anyone without Dr. Urry's local knowledge most of the entries would be quite baffling. '*Terra que est juxta magnam stratam*' (for which Johannes Dodekere paid 19 shillings per annum in 1200) a tyro with a certain minimum of monk-Latin might rightly connect with an address in the main street, and with or without the gift of tongues, he might identify 'Wenchiape' with Wincheap; but what would he make of Andresgate, Ritherchiape, Salthelle, Bagberri or Hethenmannelane? If he gave the correct answers—The Parade, Dover Street, Lower Bridge Street, New Ruttington Lane and Stour Street, then he must certainly have been taking a peep at Dr. Urry's maps.

Given that *venella* means 'Lane', the identification of *Venella Sancti Johannis* as St. John's Lane, near the Municipal Buildings, is easy enough. Now an unpretentious link enabling you to get from the Employment Exchange or the Weights and Measures Office to Castle Street, it was, we find, already a part of the road-pattern in 1166, and its name is the last visible link with the lost church of St. John. In Hitler's war the *Venella Sancti Johannis* of the monastic rentals suffered from the hostile attention of 'the enemies of God and Christ', so that a bit later archaeologists went a-prodding and proved that it was sitting on the unsuspected remains of a prehistoric civilisation. How this one little road can gather together the loose strands of the centuries and knit them into one pattern!

The names and the occupations of the monks' tenants are quite fascinating. Eudo, Odbold and Wiulph, for instance, have a distinctly mediaeval ring about them, as do Mariotta, Diriva and Brithtiua; others are the familiar Johns, Richards, Thomases and Williams, further identified by the places they came from, their occupations or their fathers' names; and the Agneses, Matildas, Cecilias, Christinas and Emmas are usually the wife or widow of some named man. Rohesia is a Norman girl—Becket's sister. But what would be the race of Lieviva, Gunnild, Eadrun or Atheliza?

The trades and professions of the tenants remind us of the source of many of our present-day surnames, the commonest being priest and clerk; 'doctor' or 'moneyer' are not perhaps usual family names, but any telephone directory will show plenty of names in the food and drink group as recorded in the rentals: cook, butler, baker and miller; even more in the construction industry: mason, carpenter, glazier, plumber, painter and thatcher; and in the clothing and footwear section: weaver, dyer, webb, fuller, mercer, tailor, skinner, tanner, shoemaker and glover.

The centre of gravity of the town in the twelfth century, as in the twentieth, lay within the ancient walls, where most of the streets were already on the alignments we know so well today. Outside the boundaries of the town centre there were suburbs lining Northgate, Westgate and Wincheap, just as they do at present. It is all so familiar that if a modern citizen could be transported by some time-machine back to twelfth-century Canterbury he would have little difficulty in finding his way about. If he had a house or a shop he might well find that the piece of ground on which it was built was already, in the twelfth century, divided off as a separate unit of ownership. There are many plots of land of which this could be said, in Wincheap, Northgate, Lower Bridge Street, St. Peter's Street and Stour Street. To take an example, at the corner of St. Peter's Lane and the street of that name is the sign of 'The Kentish Cricketers'. If the licensee could be induced to patronise our time-machine he would have the pleasure of bidding good cheer to Goldere the clerk, son of Elias Cat, who some 800 years ago paid rent to the monks for the exact plot on which this excellent hostelry is now built.

In cellars and basements in the High Street, Burgate and Palace Street remains of twelfth-century houses can still be seen. Although at least thirty of them were stone-built, nothing remains above ground. The rest were wooden framed and roofed with thatch, so that with precautions no doubt at a minimum, the city was ravaged by fire at frequent intervals.

At the same time the first shoots of the tender plant of self-government were beginning to show. The men who ruled Canterbury for the king had been described—officially that is—by various titles (praepositus, prefect, portgarefa amongst others), but in the time of Henry II they were called reeves, and there were two of them. Then came two changes; first the joint office became elective, and secondly the name 'bailiff' was adopted to describe it. It seems that this election business was at first a little bit irregular, but in the reign of Henry II's grandson, Henry III, the right was confirmed and the practice was placed firmly on a legal basis.

Another step forward was the development, from a Saxon-type local court, the Burghmote, of the embryo of an executive body. Although it carried on with its judicial duties, if that is not too grand a word for its activities, it started to grow an administrative arm like a wounded crab developing a new claw. It was this new arm that turned eventually into the medieval Common Council of the city, and was accordingly the ancestor of the modern city council. But in the twelfth century there was no fiddle-faddle with written summonses to the meetings; the Burghmote horn was sounded in the several quarters of the city to announce the sessions; three feet of curving brass with a bell mouth and moulded mouthpiece, and bearing the riveted patch of some long-ago repair, it is a difficult instrument for the modern civic executant to master. Its use is, for this and other reasons, strictly limited; its two-note unmelodious blast presages a speech by the Right Worshipful the Mayor; but seven or eight hundred years ago it played an indispensable part in the government of the city.

As evidence becomes more plentiful, dates are apt to fall so thick and fast as to become a bore; there is however one date in Canterbury's history that is as important as it is easy to remember 1234 (one, two, three, four) was the date of Henry III's charter confirming liberties, including those already taken of electing bailiffs. It also gave Canterbury greater financial independence by what was termed a grant of the city in fee farm to the citizens. By this technical-sounding mediaeval ploy the locals were enabled to compound with the king for the feudal dues, the collection of which gave the sheriff of Kent an excuse to come prying into their affairs. The king said, in effect, 'You collect amongst yourselves £X, hand that over by equal instalments at Easter and Michaelmas, and I'll tell my sheriff to keep out.' To be specific, the sum that Canterbury had to pay was £60 per annum, but that was not the end of the matter. The Crown had taken on sundry obligations which the city was now expected to assume as part of the bargain; one of these was a payment of twenty marks annually to the Leper Hospital at Harbledown, which Henry II had promised as part of his penance for the murder of Becket. This disbursement (£13 6s. 8d. in the old money, and now £13.33), is still made each year out of the city rates. Is there any other record of the ransom of a king's soul being decimalised? We doubt it.

The list of prefects or praepositi goes back to 780 when, as a result of his being mentioned in legal documents, we hear of one Aldhun, but as in the case of some of Canterbury's other institutions, there are many gaps. Hlothwig is mentioned late in the tenth century and Aelfword had the ill-fortune to become a

P.O.W. when the Danes sacked Canterbury in 1011. In the year of the Norman Conquest, Bruman got a black mark for unjust exaction. Even at that early period the predecessors of Mr. Mayor were both literally and metaphorically in the wars, a tradition which was later to be revived at all-too-frequent intervals, as will appear. There is now the exciting possibility that a complete list of the names of these men may be recovered from a source not hitherto explored; Canterburians will await the result with interest.

Neither the bailiffs of Canterbury nor the citizens were in any way subservient to the two great ecclesiastical houses, Christ Church and St. Augustine, whose money and influence must have pervaded the whole life of the place. From time to time there were spectacular riots, routs and fights between the rank and file of Town and Cowl. Perhaps one such is worth relating because of the unusual weapon used; in a fracas concerning the sale of fish, a monk received a painful slap in the face from a 'halybut'. Every now and then there would be a show-down between the Corporation and one or other of the Monasteries; the parties went into all the disputes and differences between them and arranged some compromise, which they then embodied in a voluminous legal document.

When the monks of Christ Church so carefully prepared their rental in 1166, Thomas Becket was still alive and the cathedral was still the Cathedral of Anselm. The Choir, the Nave and the Towers as they now exist had yet to be built. In the city outside none of the great mediaeval monuments had yet come into being: the Black and Grey friaries, the Poor Priests' Hospital and that of St. Thomas (naturally); the mighty Westgate.

Dr. Urry has done his work so well that a good deal of the detective expertise and theorising with which authors of books about ancient places like to entertain their readers is quite superfluous in Canterbury, and we are deprived of a certain amount of pleasurably hopeful travelling by having arrived at the answer almost before we have started.

As distinct from the buildings, the streets of Canterbury have changed little since the twelfth century. A departure from, or addition to, the layout of 1200 is the exception rather than the rule. But what of the gentle Stour? Have its devious channels stayed unaltered for the last 800 years? They have changed more, it seems, than the roads and streets. In the rush to seize the benefits that flowing water brings in a primitive community, the twelfth-century men opened up new cuts and made diversions of the river; some of these outlived their usefulness and have now disappeared completely.

When the Romans reorganised Belgic Durwhern into Roman Durovernum it is pretty certain that they built it to the south-east of the mainstream of the river, and that the secondary branch that now flows through the heart of the city was artificially cut in Saxon times. The new channel certainly proved its worth, and attracted to its banks several mills, some long forgotten, but two that have left their names. King's Bridge, which links the High Street to St. Peter's Street receives its name from King's Mill that used to adjoin it, while Abbot's Mill, formerly the property of St. Augustine's, survived into living memory; the dam and sluices and the axle of the mill-wheel are still there to see, and Mill Lane, if these are ever removed, will preserve the memory. What Prior Wibert's waterworks did for his monastery, the River Stour could, to some extent at least, do for those lucky enough to have it flowing past their doors. The founders of the mediaeval hospitals and friaries were not likely to overlook this point, and as time went on their buildings almost filled up the gaps between the mills.

First came the Hospital of St. Thomas, or Eastbridge Hospital. Different accounts are given of the origin of this really fascinating building, or rather group of buildings, which like mediaeval Canterbury itself spans the centuries, from the pure Norman Romanesque undercroft to the colour television set that the latest benefactor has provided in the recreation room. As we have seen at the cathedral, after Becket's martyrdom building was beginning to show the influence of the Gothic style with the pointed arch. It is known that Eastbridge Hospital was founded for the accommodation of poor pilgrims, and on seeing its Romanesque architecture the earnest seeker for the truth would be excused for thinking that the hospital was built before Becket's time, and that he had found a haunt of the pilgrims coming to see the shrines of Alphege and Dunstan, the great Saxon saints. This would indeed be exciting, but cooler and more knowledgeable critics tell us that the undercroft is of the same period as the refectory above, which is undoubtedly in the incipient Gothic style of the late twelfth century. It seems that it was not an uncommon practice at the beginning of the vogue for Gothic architecture for the undercroft of a building to be built in the earlier style. So the pre-Becket theory collapses.

The hospital has an enormous chest which once contained its archives. What secrets, what ancient gossip, what sidelights of social conditions they must conceal; this little hospital is a typical Canterbury sideshow and would attract the inquirer and detain him for months if not years if he yielded to his antiquarian curiosity. Those who have not months, let alone years to spare, might prevail on the Master to let them indulge in a literary *degustation* of a representative selection of the hospital's documents; he might come up with the following archivistical menu which was the hospital's contribution to a recent collation of records:

Item—the grant (about 1180) of land to the Hospital by John, son of Vivian, provost of the City of Canterbury, the father having unloaded the land on his sons before setting off for the Crusades nearly thirty years before.

Item—another grant by Ralph, the son of Arnold of Eastbridge, in consideration of fourteen marks which will free him from 'the Jews into whose hands have fallen the said land and all my other lands and possessions'.

Item—Archbishop Parker's rules for the Hospital, made in 1569, requiring a school to be kept for boys where they be taught to read and to write beautifully.

Item—letters patent of George II, confirming a dispensation for plurality granted by the Archbishop of Canterbury. The date, 1753, shows that this must have been Archbishop Herring, one of the less good Primates about whom there will be more anon.

To condense the story that these archives tell we find that after many vicissitudes the institution was re-founded by Archbishop Whitgift in the reign of Elizabeth I for housing old people, and that is still its use. Earlier the pilgrims are thought to have used the crypt as a dormitory. In addition to the dormitory and refectory there is upstairs a chapel of the thirteenth century with Decorated windows; then in the seventeenth century a wing was built which extends over the river; an almost waterline view can be seen from a window in the crypt. Another view of the gliding waters is through an opening in the floor of the room where the inmates watch their colour-television. Referred to by the Master of the Hospital as his 'oubliette', this sinister feature was discovered in the course of alterations; a glass window and guard-rail provide against unfortunate accidents.

Anyone following up the tale of Lambin Frese, the moneyer whose sparks may have, indirectly, burnt down half the cathedral in 1174, would be curious to see the place to which he moved his potentially incendiary operations. They would find Lamblane (as it was called, echoing his Christian name, when Frese lived there) rechristened Stour Street, and his old plot occupied by a building erected long after Frese's time but still ancient, the Poor Priests' Hospital. It seems that Frese's son, Roger, sold out to one Alexander of Gloucester, a philanthropist, who founded the hospital about 1200. Between Lambin and Roger, if it is not too much of a digression to mention it, there was an interregnum when a remarkable character called Adam of Charing held the property. Remarkable, overworked epithet, is almost inadequate to describe one who seems to have combined the positions of wealthy Kentish landowner and shop-steward in the Seamen's Union. A Becket-hater, he made trouble when the archbishop was trying to escape from England; he prevailed on the mariners to turn back to port by warning them that they and their families would probably be victimised by an enraged king if they helped Becket to elude the royal clutches.

Like the Eastbridge Hospital, the Poor Priests' has a history sufficiently long, varied and interesting to fill a whole volume. Since its original use was discontinued in the time of Elizabeth I, the building has done duty at various times as a Bluecoat School, bridewell (or gaol), workhouse, furniture depository, organ-building factory, ambulance brigade headquarters, city health department and the military museum of The Buffs. It is a roughly L-shaped stone-and-flint building dating from 1376. Architecturally, its most impressive features are the king-post roof of the former refectory, the framework of which is a magnificent piece of mediaeval carpentry, and the gable with cupola, clock and traceried window, which doubtless dates from the fourteenth century.

In the Buffs museum, old soldiers fuss lovingly over rows of identical medals that the regiment has won, the home-made pop-gun captured from the Mau-Mau, old-time Buffs' uniforms, and spirited but highly unrealistic prints of some of the innumerable battles in which the regiment distinguished itself. To the over-sophisticated perhaps a load of old military junk; but an Aladdin's cave to the elderly officers who come to potter and relive their campaigns, and to the relations of the fallen who perhaps browse around and shed a tear.

No sooner had the hospitals of Eastbridge and the Poor Priests been established than Canterbury was invaded by the adherents of a new religious ideal, the friars Black, White and Grey. They were recruited, from about 1200, to fill a role which neither the secular priests nor the monks seemed particularly anxious to play, that of taking the gospel to the people; and to follow a mode of life which had little appeal to the well-fed inhabitants of the monasteries, one of poverty and humility.

In the new commercial area between St. George's Street and Gravel Walk developers are building a modern shopping complex which they call 'The Whitefriars Development', and since there is no physical remnant above ground of the Augustinian Friary, the name of this trading enterprise is the last observable vestige of these Friars in Canterbury. But buildings of the Grey and Black Friars still stand beside the little river.

In 1224 Francesco Bernardone, better known as St. Francis of Assisi, appointed the leader of the first party of Grey Friars (who were also known as Franciscan Minorite or Barefoot Friars) to come to England. When the friars appeared at Canterbury the monks of Christ Church did not see the mission as implying any shortcoming in themselves; they entertained them hospitably, if perhaps a little condescendingly. Having hitch-hiked from the Continent in rags and without a penny the visitors must have been duly grateful. They decided to split up; five were to go on to Oxford, and four to stay and set up shop in Canterbury. A member of the Canterbury contingent, Thomas Eccleston, was one of those historically useful people who keep journals. After telling how they lodged as a temporary arrangement in the Poor Priests' Hospital, he writes: 'Soon after this they were granted the use of a small room underneath the school house. In this they sat almost all day with the door shut. When the boys had gone in the evening they went into the schoolroom.'

In view of the claims and counter-claims about the antiquity of certain Canterbury schools, the fact that in the year of grace 1224 there was a school within the purlieus of the Poor Priests' Hospital is worth remembering. It is surprising however to hear the claim advanced that it was Oxford that received the first Franciscan settlement in England. Someone must have forgotten to send a copy of Eccleston's journal to the Bodleian.

The Eastbridge branch of the River Stour forms an elongated

island between itself and the mainstream running in front of the Westgate. Behind the Poor Priests' Hospital the Eastbridge branch itself divides to form an island within an island, and over the further channel, supported on pillars rising from the bed of the stream, is the one remaining building of the Franciscans' permanent settlement. This ancient stone-and-flint building, with its roof of mellow red tiles and with its arch-supported gable mirrored in the smooth waters of the slowly moving stream, is a favourite subject for snapshots and postcards. No one really knows what its function was in the friary. It may have been the dormitory; on the other hand it may not. It has many times been altered and restored since the dissolution of the convent, but the scars have long since been hidden by the patina of time. Today, in the heart of a thriving and prosperous city, the melancholy and sequestered air of a backwater hangs around the place; the untidy backs of buildings in Stour Street, an incongruous telephone exchange, the picturesque but far-from-orderly rear of the Eastbridge Hospital, a dilapidated bridge half thirteenth century, half staringly modern, and the ramshackle sheds of a market garden reinforce the air of forlorn melancholy. Back land, tucked away behind everything else, and in the thirteenth century probably marshy and smelly to boot, this is typical of the places chosen by these humble followers of the Gospel for their habitations.

The story of the friaries is very much a part of Canterbury's history as a city. It was probably no accident that the Black and Grey Friaries were in the midst of the town well away from the cathedral because, as this physical fact well illustrates, the founders of the orders were not satisfied with the accepted idea of the Church as an embattled institution resisting under the leadership of the Pope the assaults of the devil; they preferred to dwell rather on the duty of taking the Gospel message out into the highways and byways for the people to hear. The powerful supporters of the church militant were the great landowners and feudal bigwigs, but it was the despised bourgeoisie, mayors, sheriffs, rich tradesmen and prosperous artisans who took the friars to their capacious bosoms. Alas, this very prosperity was the undoing of the orders. Within a century and a half, the friaries had been extended, remodelled and embellished, and had become the burial places of the rich, who showered them with gifts and legacies. This good fortune was fatal to the virtues of the friars, and the gaunt beggar with his patched tunic, who landed penniless at Dover and won the sympathy of the people for his simplicity, degenerated into the oily covetous con-man of Chaucer's Tales. However, that is a long tale which ended in 1538 when Henry VIII suppressed the friaries, and it is only due to the innate conservatism of Canterbury that we have inherited, even if in a somewhat mutilated state, two of the Blackfriars' buildings. We need not shed too many tears over the fact that the Dominican guest-house on the left bank of the branch of the river has few, if any, of its original features left; the important thing is that it has survived, changed perhaps but still recognisable. A building that has been through the hands of so many owners since the friars were evicted, and been put to so many and various uses—it functioned long ago both as a weaving-shed and as a meeting-hall for the Walloons, and has been a refectory for art students and the headquarters of a Scout troop in our own time—must of necessity have been hacked about at one time or another. In effect, its owners have regarded it as a useful building, coming in handy for meeting various social needs, rather than as a museum exhibit, and for this reason we still have it. Dominic de Guzman, otherwise St. Dominic, would have approved (what he would have had to say about the use of the refectory, on the other bank, as a Christian Science Church we do not know—the question is too deep for light discussion). Time has preserved most of the thirteenth-century windows, and the curious recess in the former dining-room in which was mounted the pulpit from which one of the brethren read passages from the scriptures while his colleagues consumed their victuals. With the river between, and the bower of stately trees around them, the two buildings give to this corner of Canterbury a pleasing blend of nature and history. The appearance would be improved if the Christian Scientists did not find it necessary to announce their presence with intrusive lettering on the flank wall of their old buildings, and even more so if something could be done about the enormous collection of second-hand motor vehicles which disfigure the foreground between the guest house of the Dominicans and the street that is still called 'The Friars'.

Of Canterbury's ancient parish churches only one, St. Mildred's, is built anywhere near the King's Bridge branch of the river. Its dedication suggests that it is probably of venerable age, as one cannot imagine a Norman dedicating, or allowing to be dedicated,

A Norman tower of the cathedral

any church to a Saxon saint. Mildred was the great-great-granddaughter of King Ethelbert himself, and the style of construction of the nave, with its unusually massive quoin-stones, backs up the general evocation of Saxon-dom.

That the church was there in Lanfranc's time is shown by the story of his quarrel with the monks of St. Augustine's. They did not like the new abbot whom the archbishop wanted to foist on them, threatened to go on strike and were locked out instead; they trooped round to St. Mildred's church, no doubt to consider what came next. The answer was 'dinner time'; they felt very hungry, and so decided to go back—on Lanfranc's terms.

Standing practically in the shadow of the keep of Canterbury Castle, the church was, in times of old when the castle was used as a gaol, a place of sanctuary for escaped prisoners, and most conveniently sited for such a purpose. The trembling wretch would be lectured by the coroner—a much more important figure in those days than in our own—and given by virtue of the protection of the Holy Church the option, instead of going to the gallows, the stake or whatever other punishment his crime entailed, of clearing out of England and becoming an outlaw. In times slightly less ferocious, though still troubled, (in 1626 to be precise), the Father of Angling, Isaak Walton, was himself hooked, gaffed and landed at this little church—by Mrs. Walton.

Canterbury's medieval parish churches are very much a wasting asset. Of the twenty-two known to have existed in 1200, eleven have disappeared completely; of two, the tower only remains; among the rest, Holy Cross is deconsecrated and to be used for welfare services, St. Margaret's is assigned to the deaf of the diocese, while uncertainty surrounds the future of St. Alphege's, St. Peter's, and even, sad to relate, St. Martin's.

Holy Cross, Sudbury built when he re-edified the Westgate; it replaced a small chapel on the old gate; the other churches are much older, but have all been in various degrees scrubbed out, tidied up, disinfected and modernised by the Victorian ecclesiologists, without however quite destroying their cosy medieval atmosphere, which lingers most pleasantly at St. Peter's and St. Alphege's.

St. Dunstan's has two special claims to distinction; the tomb of the Roper family where the head of Sir Thomas More is buried, and the memory, four hundred years older, of Henry II's call when he made his great penance in 1174. Riding down from

6

Eastbridge Hospital

Harbledown in full panoply, with mail-clad warriors and streaming standards, Henry paused at St. Dunstan's, went within, and changed into the garb of a humble penitent pilgrim, in which he walked barefoot to the distant cathedral. So many hundreds of strokes from the rods of the bishops, abbots and monks did he receive that we are surprised to hear that he was able to ride away the next day, fully absolved, and carrying with him the pilgrim's phial of water mixed with the martyr's blood.

The street to which St. Peter's church gives its name runs from the King's Bridge to the Westgate, the little church being set back on the right, the path to its porch threading a tiny garden. It is much too old to have documents about its foundation; those of the twelfth century speak of it as already part of the Canterbury scene; the non-expert at any rate, wonders whether, as at St. Mildred's, the large quoin-stones of the little square tower might be Saxon. The interior has certainly kept its ancient flavour, which seems by some magic to flow out through the porch, down the path and into the street, which stays obstinately medieval despite the growing proportion of more modern buildings among the ancient ones. There are little irregularities in the alignment of the frontages within a subtle curve to the left; the vista is closed in by the great mass of the Westgate, which splendid gateway was designed to be ruggedly strong in defence, but also to be pleasing to the eye as well from the back as from the front; it keeps St. Peter's Street snug and protected and intimate, as a medieval street should be. It is solidly built in Kentish rag, and the stylish way in which the sixty-foot-high drum towers are given moulded string courses with subtle offsets to relieve their complete plainness, and the crisp assurance with which the Gothic gateway with its square frame, and the machicolation above are worked into the design as seen from the front, and the guard-house and lookout turrets are smoothly incorporated—all this betokens the work of a great architect, and makes its attribution to Henry Yevele almost certain.

The bailiffs of Canterbury in 1377 when the gate was built must have wished that they could claim the honour and glory of such an achievement, but in fact it was the Archbishop, Simon of Sudbury, who was responsible. Richard II's reign was a time of great unrest; the whole countryside of Kent was seething with discontent and Simon took it upon himself to see that the defences of the city were in good shape. The fact that he already had the rebuilding of the nave of the cathedral on his hands did not deter this energetic and civic-minded prelate; but unfortunately the Westgate and other defences that he constructed proved to be a kind of Maginot Line; when Wat Tyler's revolt broke out, soon after the fortifications had been completed, the Canterbury mob let the rebels into the city, and all hell broke loose in an orgy of burning and slaying. The archbishop, who was also Chancellor and held responsible for the hated poll-tax, one of the causes of the rebellion, was in London, which the insurgents now proceeded to invade. The government must have been completely demoralised; Sudbury was not safe, even when guarded by men-at-arms and archers in the Tower. The mob dragged him out and, with eager and inexpert hacks, beheaded him on Tower Hill. If it is any consolation to his shade, it can be said that as long as the Westgate stands his name will always be remembered in Canterbury. And the same cannot be said of *all* archbishops.

Until the Reform Act the jurisdiction of the city ended at the Westgate. The manor of that name outside the city walls was one of several precincts, vills and boroughs within the circuit of the city where its writ did not run, and became a favourite dumping-ground for unwanted paupers in course of their removal to their home parishes in the county of Kent. The Westgate itself, though it failed to keep Wat Tyler out, was well adapted to keep wrongdoers in, and after little more than a century it began its career as a prison which continued until well into the nineteenth century. Paris has lost its Bastille, Oxford its Bocardo, but Canterbury's Westgate survives, as a museum of arms, armour, constables' staves and so forth, and also as the city's Chamber of Horrors, with the condemned cell as the climax to a showing of fetters, manacles and gyves, and the old gallows tree. It is by far the most popular of Canterbury's many museums.

Beyond is St. Dunstan's, running up the gentle hill to the church on the left, where the London Road branches off. This magnificent street grows on you. Small houses on a wide road do not impress dramatically at first; their significance must sink in. There are thirteen successive gables of ancient buildings; not strictly medieval perhaps, but up to three or even four hundred years old. Even forgetting the church itself and the mighty Westgate (if that were possible) St. Dunstan's can show the seventeenth century House of Agnes, traditionally identified as the one Dickens had in mind when he described the home of

Agnes Wickfield in *David Copperfield*. The Falstaff Hotel, a little older, the Tudor Roper Gateway, which once led to the house of Margaret, Sir Thomas More's favourite and faithful daughter, and the Georgian Westgate House.

The traveller coming down the hill towards the city has before him Yevele's masterpiece, looking down this avenue of architectural wonder, while away to his left front, rising above the huddled roofs of the city, the cathedral rises in all its stateliness. This is a panorama that any other city of the land would find it hard to equal.

The cathedral and city owe much to the Priors of Christ Church, especially to those outstanding men who rebuilt, extended and beautified the several parts of the great church and its monastery. Wilbert, of waterworks fame, Ernulf and Conrad, linked together as the rebuilders of the Norman Choir, Henry of Eastry—the Harry of 'Bell Harry'—who ruled for forty-seven years during the reigns of the first three Edwards, and Thomas Chillenden, 'the greatest builder of a prior that ever was in Christes church' according to Leland's well-known description. There may be others who could compete for the title of the greatest Prior, William Sellinge for instance, who caught the influence of the Renaissance and brought back from Italy much Latin and Greek learning to Canterbury. But the verdict of Leland is commonly accepted. Chillenden's works are too numerous to mention, but undoubtedly the greatest of them was the rebuilding of the nave.

The great wealth of Christ Church had been poured out unsparingly to uphold and better supply with devotional objects and robes the great cathedral church, but by the 1370s the priors and archbishops found themselves faced with a task for which even that opulence was insufficient—the rebuilding of Lanfranc's nave, so ruinous that it could no longer be allowed to stand without reconstruction. When John Finch was prior the work was put in hand, but so great was the task that the archbishop, Simon of Sudbury, set up a building fund quite in the modern style, with the valuable difference that he was able to offer an indulgence of forty days to all good people who contributed to the work. But Sudbury had not made much progress when his career was cut short by Wat Tyler's rebels.

The task of designing the new nave brought into the story of

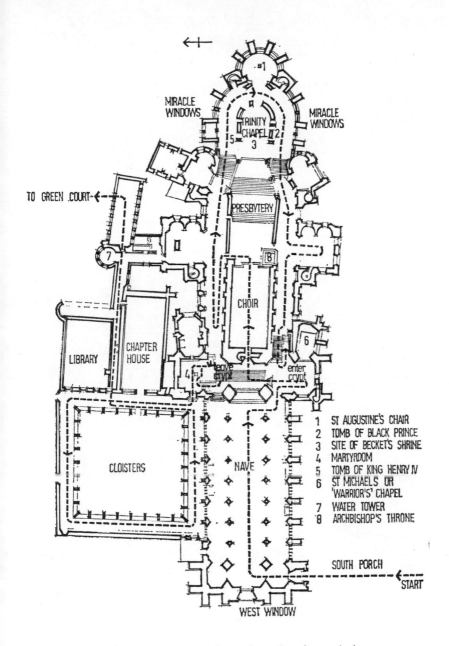

Plan of the Cathedral (reprinted from the *Pilgrim's Guide*, by courtesy of the Corporation of Canterbury). The broken line is a suggested route for visitors.

the cathedral one of the most distinguished names in English architecture. Henry Yevele may or may not have designed the Westgate, but it is certain that he was the architect of the nave of Canterbury Cathedral, although as recently as thirty years ago the fact was not generally known. It is strange, for example, to note that in a standard work on Canterbury Cathedral—the *Memorials* of Woodruff and Danks published in 1912—there is no reference at all to Yevele, and in fact the authors seem to have been ignorant of any connection between this architect and the cathedral. They imply the contrary by stating that the designer of the nave had probably been trained at Gloucester, which would not be true of Yevele. He was in effect the central government's architect in charge of the whole of the south of England, and is well known for his work on the nave of Westminster Abbey, and on the reconstruction of Westminster Hall. One cannot find in the *Encyclopaedia Britannica* even today any reference to this architect. Like his contemporary, Geoffrey Chaucer, he would frequently have to come to Canterbury in the course of his duties and there is every probability that the two men were familiar acquaintances, if not friends. Whether the city walls needed repair, or the castle was due for renovation, those responsible were told to work under the direction of Master Yevele, while Geoffrey, as a member of Parliament for Kent, a justice of the peace and guardian of two Kentish wards, would often be a visitor to the county and its premier city.

The Perpendicular style in which Yevele reconstructed the nave had never before been seen in south-east England, although something like it had been used at Gloucester a good fifty years earlier. Different opinions have been expressed about the merits of the design, depending on whether the critic is writing before or after it was discovered that Yevele was the architect. Woodruff, in the *Memorials*, after commenting that the architectural effect of Chillenden's nave suffers from the narrowness of the structure in proportion to its height, an effect which is most apparent in the side aisles, goes on to quote the opinion of another author to the following effect: 'No reflection of religious zeal can be discerned in the architectural expression of the naves of Winchester and Canterbury. Rather must we see in them the tomb of the religious sentiment of art as their ordered and scientific panelling, first overlaid and then wiped out of existence the architecture of faith.' Whatever may be the meaning of this mystical approach to architectural criticism, would it ever have been offered, one wonders, if the author had known that he was speaking of the work of Henry Yevele? To the layman, the pretentious nonsense about the architecture of faith smacks of the affectation of the modern environmentalist poseur. Yevele's biographer, John H. Harvey, has no similar reservations; to him the nave of Canterbury is the very finest product of English Gothic, the finest interior now remaining in England, and one of the greatest masterpieces of art in the world. It is of course quite true that it is narrow compared with, say, the nave of Rheims or York. Apart from the fact that the rebuilding was carried out on the same ground plan as the old, namely the nave of Lanfranc, it must be remembered that at Canterbury the nave and the choir are very much more two separate entities than in the two great cathedrals mentioned above. The two parts of the cathedral are neither on the same level or even on the same precise alignment, and they form as it were two churches end-on-end rather than one single great structure, albeit divided functionally, as are York and Rheims and many other mighty cathedrals. We therefore have virtually two buildings of moderate but impressive size rather than one single stupendous architectural form, and it is the achievement of Yevele to make the nave, in spite of its far from ample width, the striking and magnificent piece of architecture that it is.

With the nave were rebuilt the western transepts. The south-western of these is noteworthy for more than its architecture; it contains St. Michael's Chapel, long known as the Warriors' Chapel from the memorials of military men preserved there, but now famous the world over as the great shrine of The Buffs, the Third Foot, the regiment whose exploits are remembered at the military museum in the Poor Priests' Hospital and whose dead are commemorated every week-day morning by the ceremony of the turning, in this chapel, of a page of the book in which their names are recorded.

One is not exactly enticed into the chapel; sometimes the opening in the barrier is shut, and with the hanging flags, and the drums, lectern and the large tomb taking most of the floor space, an unseen 'no-entry' sign seems to register, quite unnecessarily as it happens, on most people's minds.

Anyone who does not go into the Warriors' Chapel will probably never find out that beneath the altar is the tomb of

Stephen Langton, the Archbishop who took a leading part in getting King John to accept Magna Carta in 1215, and in fact was largely responsible for the drafting of the Charter. The tomb of Langton projects through the east wall and the protrusion can be seen from the outside; and thereby hangs a curious tale. Two great nobles were once buried in the cathedral—John, Earl of Somerset and his nephew, Thomas, Duke of Clarence—in 1410 and 1421 respectively. These two were the successive husbands of Margaret Holland, daughter of the Earl of Kent, and they were buried in St. Thomas's Chapel. The Dowager Duchess, however, wanted a more stately memorial for herself and her two husbands in a more prominent spot, and she was allowed to have St. Michael's Chapel rebuilt and a splendid marble tomb with alabaster effigies of herself and her husbands prepared. The whole of this work was finished in December of 1439 and so good was the timing that it needed but eleven days before the Duchess passed from this life in a convent at Bermondsey. A royal mandate was obtained to exhume her two husbands and to re-inter them with her in St. Michael's Chapel. In order to alter the chapel to take this very large and impressive *ménage à trois* it was necessary to disturb the tomb of Stephen Langton. His coffin was placed under the altar of the new chapel above ground, as at present; and so that it could be placed east and west without sticking out too far from the altar it was necessary to have the foot of the coffin projecting through the eastern wall. Thus was the repose of one of the greatest men that England ever produced, whose efforts have safeguarded indirectly the liberties of hundreds of millions throughout the civilised world, disturbed so that an ambitious widow, who so far as is known had made no contribution to the world's progress, could have a suitably ostentatious memorial.

The north-west is better known as the Martyrdom transept. It was here that Thomas Becket was murdered, although only the outer walls remain of the building as it was in Becket's time. An inscription cut into the stones of the wall in modern times is the only sign to show where the archbishop was murdered.

Apart from the rebuilding (completed about 1459) of the south-western tower (known within the precincts as the 'Oxford Steeple' because of its connection with Archbishop Chichele, founder of All Souls), the last great work to be carried out before the Reformation and the dissolution of the monastery was the rebuilding of 'Bell Harry'. Most of the work was carried out under the auspices of Prior Sellinge some time between 1470 and 1500. Just before Sellinge died in 1494 he had been writing to Archbishop Morton about the form of the pinnacles, which suggests that the tower was approaching completion. It is from his letter that we know that the architect was John Wastell, who was later to be employed on the erection of King's College Chapel, Cambridge. However, the tower is considered to be of a style considerably earlier in date than the period in which it was erected, and it is probable that Wastell worked upon plans and drawings prepared when the work was first mooted nearly forty years before the building was started in earnest. National disasters and famine and disease put a stop for the moment to ambitious building works. Although working on somebody else's plans, Wastell produced a masterpiece which is considered to be the finest Perpendicular-style tower in existence. The artistry is not merely in the exterior, but extends to the magnificent fan vaulting of the ceiling, 130 feet from the floor beneath the tower, and within fifty-three feet of the roof.

In a portrait one cannot linger for ever on one feature of the subject, however striking and however beautiful, or the picture will be either overloaded with detail, or never completed, or both. There can be no attempt, for instance, to describe the numerous tombs in the cathedral; those of archbishops alone would supply a perhaps wearisome catalogue, even though Henry VIII and his minions got rid of quite a few, including not only Becket's but also those of the two famous Saxon saints, Dunstan and Alphege; there are over half of the ninety-nine deceased Primates still resting somewhere in and around the building. For one cause or another no monument earlier than the thirteenth century has survived. If, in deference to the respect due to so many great churchmen, we have to select at least one of their monuments for mention, then Henry Chichele is perhaps our man; he founded All Souls, Oxford, and the College keeps his tomb in repair; it is famous, moreover, for its macabre form, with the Archbishop in full canonicals above, and his almost naked 'cadaver' below. Then, on the north side of Trinity Chapel we have royalty, who cannot be overlooked, in the persons of Henry IV and his wife Joan of Navarre in an alabaster sarcophagus, and they in turn are far outshone in fame by the Black Prince on the other side of the chapel.

Edward of Woodstock, son of King Edward III, was Prince

of Wales, but his father outlived him and the Black Prince never became King. His exploits are too well known to need retelling, but the battle of Poitiers surely represents the high-water mark of crushing victories won against fantastic odds; it left the opposing king a prisoner of war in the prince's hands, and good for almost unlimited money and political concessions by way of ransom.

Yet this stern victor had in his character softer traits, which included a particular affection for Canterbury Cathedral and a tender feeling for his cousin Joan, the Fair Maid of Kent. He endowed a chantry in the crypt of the cathedral, and paid for the formation of the beautiful Chapel of Our Lady Undercroft, where he wished to be buried. His funeral in 1376 was one of the most impressive events ever to take place in Canterbury, but the country would not hear of his being buried as modestly as he had wished and therefore he was interred beside the shrine of England's most famous martyr in the Trinity Chapel. The monument is itself remarkable in two ways. It is first of all one of the most splendid monumental memorials in England and the brass life-sized effigy of the dead man is thought to be a portrait; and secondly, the tomb is famous for the display of the Prince's helm, crest, coat-of-arms, gauntlets, shield, swordsheath and belt, which after hanging over the tomb for centuries are now in a glass case nearby, their place over the tomb being taken by carefully made replicas.

As so often happens, the fire-eating man of steel the Black Prince had a son Richard, who was by comparison soft and spine-less. After his grandfather's long reign the grandson came to the throne as Richard II; after a promising start as a boy king, he alienated the support of many powerful men and was in the end deposed and murdered. The man who supplanted him was none other than Bolingbroke, otherwise Henry IV. Perhaps Henry may have wished to placate the angry ghost of Richard's father by seeking a resting-place for his own bones in Trinity Chapel at Canterbury.

We have kept until the last a feature that is in its own way no less important and inspiring than the architecture of Yevele and Wastell, no less interesting than the royal and primatial tombs, and is in the opinion of some people the most attractive and enjoyable feature of the cathedral; its unique heritage of stained glass. The more ancient suffered from vandalistic bigotry, notably that of the seventeenth-century Puritans led by the destructive fanatic Culmer, known as 'Blue Dick', but miraculously as it seems much has survived, and the windows that remain are some of the most important and interesting in western Europe. It is impossible to describe them all in detail, or adequately to describe any of them. Even the excellent books that are available, beautifully illustrated in full colour, cannot do full justice to them; they have to be seen. What makes the task of description even more difficult is the history of 'switching' the glass from one part of the Cathedral to another. For example, the magnificent series of forty-two 'genealogical' windows was mounted, in the twelfth century, to adorn the Choir, but they were put high up in the clerestory where it was difficult to see them to advantage, and most of the figures that survive have been moved to other parts of the church, particularly the west window and south-west transept. These windows each contained two figures illustrating the ancestry of Our Lord from Adam, whose delving figure is claimed as the earliest known action-picture in glass. They form a rich gallery of medieval art, and rank as one of the pictorial wonders of the world.

Another ancient series is the so-called Poor Man's Bible, which shows scenes from the Old and New Testaments side by side. The scenes are supposed to have some similarity. It is thought that the object was to instruct an illiterate populace; although there is wording round the pictures. This early glass was designed before the windows of the cathedral had stone tracery; to supply the support the tracery later gave, the glass had heavy iron rods known as armatures. Of the Poor Man's Bible, two early thirteenth-century windows in the North Choir Aisle survive, and from about the same period date the Miracle windows in the ambulatory of Trinity Chapel; these stories, illustrating some of the miracles performed at Becket's shrine or by his intercession, are set forth in sequences of action pictures very much like the modern strip cartoon. The general effect is that of a coruscating piece of jewellery, but an experience some may find enjoyable is to inspect the windows in detail with a pair of binoculars; some of the stories illustrated are most amusing.

Other charming and ancient glass is to be seen in the trefoil windows of the Choir Triforium; specially well known is the picture showing the Danes attacking Canterbury in 1011. Of much later design is the fifteenth-century 'Royal' window in the

Martyrdom transept, showing the Yorkist King Edward IV and his family.

Perhaps a sour note is introduced by the numerous windows in which the Victorians tried quite unsuccessfully to produce imitations of the ancient glass. It is only in our own time that it has been realised that modern artists in glass had better not pretend to be what they are not, and this new appreciation led to the acceptance in 1952 of windows designed by the Hungarian-born artist Bossanyi, who has an international reputation and whose work has a special and characteristic glowing effect.

NICHOLAS FAUNT

THE Archbishops of Canterbury have given a number of sad examples of the perils that go with high office; but when Nicholas Faunt assumed the mayoralty of the city in the fifteenth century he could scarcely have thought that it carried similar dangers. The burning of Cranmer and the execution of Laud were still in the future, but already Alphege had been murdered by the Danes, and Becket by de Tracy and company, whilst Sudbury had had his head hacked off (at the eighth attempt) by Wat Tyler and his rabble.

So far, no Mayor of Canterbury had suffered in like manner, but the unfortunate Faunt was to show that there is always a first time. He lived in times that were difficult for public men who wished to keep themselves straight with the authorities, because the authorities were apt to be here today and gone tomorrow; and perhaps back again the day after.

The reigning king was Edward IV, the Yorkist who had ousted the Lancastrian Henry VI; Henry was still alive and kicking, though not as vigorously as his wife, the implacable Margaret of Anjou. Edward, though energetic and brave in times of danger and action, quickly degenerated into a playboy king once peace returned. The power behind the throne was the Earl of Warwick, known as the Kingmaker, and when it gradually dawned on him that Edward was no longer prepared to go along with some of Warwick's pet schemes, he turned very nasty and ended by going over to the Lancastrians. It was at this critical and dangerous juncture that Nicholas Faunt was elected mayor of Canterbury.

The Men of Kent east of the Medway, and the Kentish Men to its west, have many fine virtues, but if one is that of political reliability they certainly have not inherited it from their medieval ancestors, amongst whom many of the well-known rebellions of

those times seem to have originated. By Faunt's time the Wat
Tyler revolt was almost century-old history, but since that event
there had been one minor and one major insurrection in the
county. The mysterious 'Bluberd the Hermit' alias Thomas
Cheyny, a fuller, had actually been captured by one of Faunt's predecessors and the citizens of Canterbury, and handed over to the
government by whom he was hanged, drawn and quartered, the
head being sent back to be placed over the Westgate.

During the time of Henry VI, and before he had been ousted
from the throne by Edward, came the much more serious affair
of Jack Cade's rebellion. Again the Mayor of Canterbury and the
citizens received a pat on the back and a selection of new
privileges for refusing the insurgents entry to the city.

Edward's reign dated from his great victory at Towton in
Yorkshire; three years later Henry was captured and put under
lock and key, and kept there until the quarrel between Edward
and the Kingmaker. The city hired soldiers, placed watches on
the gates, and paid seven shillings 'for the carriage of a great gun
from Blackheath to Canterbury, and 5s. 7d. to four armed men
for guarding the same; also eightpence for carriage of the brazen
gun from the Court-Hall to the gates of the city and back again.'
The Corporation tried to propitiate both sides with gifts; capons,
oxen, sheep and wine for the Yorkists and unspecified goodies
for the defeated Lancastrians. The city was paying out, in the
same financial year, £251 to King Edward and Mayor Faunt's
expenses for going to London to sit in council with Henry VI, the
Earl of Warwick and the Lancastrian nobility.

Faunt had always had secret Lancastrian sympathies, and he
was supported by Walter Hopton, an innkeeper, and others of the
Red Rose faction in the city, but at first he was prudent enough
to tread warily; when a party of Lancastrian soldiery threatened
the city they were bought off by bribes—to the value of
£1 13s. 4d. (Highjacking charges have gone up considerably since
those days.) Then, unluckily for Faunt's attempts to seem impartial, King Edward fled the country and took refuge in Holland
for a time; a Lancastrian character known as the Bastard Fauconberg, who commanded the fleet in the Channel, dominated
Kent, and Nicholas felt safe in openly sporting the Red Rose.
With a considerable force equipped by the city, he left Canterbury
and joined the Bastard who was threatening London.

Within months Nicholas discovered the greatness of his error, for Edward was soon back again, having managed to borrow some money from the Duke of Burgundy to pay his army. He landed at Ravenspur, defeated the Earl of Warwick at Barnet (the Kingmaker was a rotten general, it seems) and the Lancastrian army at Tewkesbury; then he came back post-haste to do a little mopping-up in Kent. The Bastard Fauconberg was duly beheaded, and then it was Faunt's turn; some say he also was beheaded, others that he received the Bluberd treatment; it can't have mattered much to him.

It had taken centuries of hard work, of chasing after kings and doing their bidding, of wheedling and persuasion and negotiation for Canterbury to obtain its civic privileges, including that of being governed by its own mayor. All these exertions seemed to have been thrown away by the imprudence of the wretched Faunt. The city lost its liberties, and it took a great deal of money, and the display of many white roses, to get them back.

Poor Faunt paid with his head for his lack of skill and judgment in the dangerous political game. Perhaps he should have taken lessons in the gentle arts of dissimilation and pliability from the archbishop, and the prior and monks of Christchurch. The Lancastrian King, Henry VI, was, we are told, a familiar figure at Canterbury, coming as a humble pilgrim to make his offering at the famous shrine in the cathedral and being received with all honour. On his last visit, the pious King was welcomed by the archbishop and the prior and convent, and ushered to High Mass to the tune of holy anthems. A bare four years later, when Henry's opponent Edward IV and his Queen were in Canterbury with the same archbishop, the news came through that the former royal pilgrim and honoured guest had been captured by his Yorkist enemies. Without, so far as is recorded, the turning of a hair, let alone any sign of compunction, the successor of Becket immediately laid on a service of thanksgiving, with a *Te Deum* and procession to the shrine. The delighted King Edward, so far from having to order anyone to be beheaded, commanded the provision, in celebration of his success, of a magnificent stained glass window in the north-west transept of the cathedral. That window remains today, and despite its unsavoury origin, is of immense historical and heraldic interest, the *pièce de résistance* being a series of portraits of Edward himself, his Queen and their children. Whether it was installed before or after the murder of the unfortunate Henry in the Tower is uncertain.

SIX

DISSOLUTION—AND AFTER

THE writing was on the wall. It had probably been there for a very long time before the monks of Christchurch, or St. Augustine's, or the Black, White and Grey Friars of Canterbury noticed it.

The moral, economic and political ingredients of an explosive mixture were being compounded by the Fates, as our monastic friends would find out in due course when someone was reckless enough to apply the necessary spark.

Even in the time of Chaucer and Prior Chillenden, when monasticism, Catholic orthodoxy and Papal authority seemed entrenched as never before, the poet was only echoing the general feelings of the laity when, in the Prologue to the *Canterbury Tales*, he depicted the Monk, Friar, Summoner and Pardoner as a quartet of scamps.

The Monk, we remember from our schooldays, was interested only in hunting.

> He yaf nat of that text a pulled hen,
> That seith, that hunters been nat holy men.

Study in the cloister, or physical work at the monastery he regarded as complete waste of time.

> How shal the world be served?
> Lat Austin have his swink[1] to him reserved.

The Friar is out to help poor sinners to heaven, but strictly on a cash basis:

> Therefore, in stede of weping and preyeres
> Men moot yeve[2] silver to the povre freres.

[1] Swink—work.
[2] Yeve—give.

All that remains of the mediaeval Greyfriars settlement

He does not dally with the poor and sick, but goes where the money is.

> He was the beste beggere in his hous.

The Summoner was tarred with the same brush—

> He wolde suffre, for a quart of wyn,
> A good felawe to have his concubyn
> A twelf-month, and excuse him atte fulle.

The Pardoner is the worst of a very bad lot:

> His walet lay biforn him in his lappe,
> Bret-ful of pardoun come from Rome al hoot, . . .

> And in a glas he hadde pigges bones . . .
> And thus, with feyned flaterye and japes,
> He made the person and the peple his apes.

Prior Chillenden, so far as we know, was no poet but a man of action, and the action he took was to build a new hostel for pilgrims, not because of a shortage of beds, but in the hope that better accommodation might attract more pilgrims, whose numbers were on the wane.

When the great humanist, Erasmus, visited Canterbury early in the sixteenth century, his contemporary, Luther, had already applied the spark to the dangerous and unstable explosives, but the ensuing conflagration had not yet spread to England. Erasmus came not as a Protestant but as a loyal Catholic, yet the monks were disappointed in the lukewarm interest he displayed in the cathedral's sacred relics. He brought with him his friend Colet, and, the reliquary cupboard having been opened, 'It is wonderful to relate', says Erasmus, 'how many bones were brought out thence, skulls, jawbones, teeth, hands, fingers and whole arms.' The cupboard was shut again, and the visitors passed on, without having seen the fragments of the table on which Jesus celebrated the Last Supper, of the oak on which Abraham climbed, and of the clay out of which God made Adam.

But they did show Erasmus an old shoe. 'This is the shoe of St. Thomas,' he was told.

'Genuine?' he asked; it certainly looked dirty enough. 'What am I supposed to do?'

'Kiss it,' he was told tersely. He did so, and the memory, not apparently a pleasant one, remained with him for a long time.

If the monks and friars of Canterbury had shown a modicum

7

The refectory of the Blackfriars monastery

of the worldliness of which their Prologue counterparts had such an excess they might, even if they could not deflect the coming cataclysm, at least have refrained from inviting it. This some of them seemed to do in the tragically farcical affair of the Holy Maid of Kent, Elizabeth Barton, a maidservant, who began about the year 1525 to have dreams and visions. Within a year her fame was such that the Archbishop of Canterbury instructed the prior of Christchurch to send two of the monks to enquire into the case. Dr. Bocking, Warden of the Christchurch Manors, was one of these; he got Elizabeth into St. Sepulchre's Nunnery at Canterbury and under his instruction her prophesies became still more remarkable. She even attracted pilgrims, who believed her to be in direct communication with the Virgin Mary. Unfortunately the prophetess's utterance began to take a more and more political slant and she declared that if Henry VIII persisted in divorcing Catherine of Aragon he should 'no longer be king of this realm and should die a villain's death.' However, it was the deluded and unfortunate woman and her collaborators, including Bocking, who suffered at Tyburn the fate which she had prophesied for Henry. Two of the Grey Friars from Canterbury were also implicated in this dangerous affair and suffered similarly.

After this unpromising prelude it is not surprising that there was no reprieve from dissolution for the Grey Friars in 1538 or for Christchurch in 1540 any more than for the other friaries in Canterbury.

The choice present for Anne Boleyn of a letter of St. Mary Magdalen written in heaven in characters of gold, could not save St. Augustine's, and there was no reprieve, either, for St. Thomas; he was demoted from his saintly status, his name expunged from the Church's calendar, his shrine destroyed, and its treasures carted off to London.

At Christchurch, more than half the monks were permitted to become members of the new foundation, the Dean and Chapter and the remainder, including the last prior, were pensioned off. At Greyfriars it is noteworthy that the surrender of the convent was received on behalf of the King by the then Bishop of Dover, Richard Ingworth. One of the original Franciscan party that came to England in 1224 was a man of the same name, Richard Ingworth.

At St. Augustine's there was to be no Dean and Chapter to

maintain the church or the monastery; the Crown kept both in its own hands and for the most part destroyed the buildings, which became a quarry for the neighbourhood, and also for the fortifications on neighbouring coasts and even in Calais. The abbot's lodgings, however, were spared and were converted into what was named the King's House, a link in a chain of staging posts between London and Dover for the King's use and that of distinguished foreign visitors. So it was that the Fyndon Gate and the guests' refectory have survived to the present time.

The Greyfriars' and Blackfriars' buildings were transferred to private hands, and it is worth recalling that the Greyfriars were at one time owned by the family of Richard Lovelace, the Cavalier Poet who wrote, 'Stone walls do not a prison make, nor iron bars a cage'.

So Henry VIII had removed overnight the attraction that had made Canterbury one of the three foremost places of pilgrimage of Europe. He had also, with equal lack of ceremony, closed for ever the doors of the two great monasteries that symbolised the city's ecclesiastical pre-eminence and brought considerable grist to its mills. If Lourdes should lose its *grotte* and Oxford its university at a blow, the combined loss could not unfairly be compared to that which fell on Canterbury between 1538 and 1540, and men may have wondered whether the city would now fade into obscurity. Yet the period of a century and a half that separated the suppression of the monasteries from the advent of William of Orange proved to be one of the most colourful in its history, and not only left a record of interesting and dramatic events, but also threw up famous characters, and ancestors of characters equally famous; literature and architecture which contribute generously to the colour of the portrait we are trying to paint; and even provided Canterbury with the most important items of its civic insignia.

The Tudor tyrant created and endowed the Dean and Chapter, and handed to them the cathedral to care for and the buildings of the monastery of Christchurch to deal with as they should wish. At the same time he made provision—the reason for use of this somewhat non-committal term will appear hereafter—for the King's School—the King being Henry himself—to supply in whole, or in part, the service which the monks had provided for the community in educating its sons.

Enough has been said in describing the present state of the monastic buildings and of the friaries to show, for better or for worse, what fate had in store for them.

Another of Henry's actions was to bequeath to the city a grim relic and a new pilgrimage. His Chancellor, Sir Thomas More, declined on grounds of conscience to take the Oath of Supremacy declaring the King to be head of the Church of England, and within months ended his career at the block. All was done in proper legal order—if one can so describe the use of perjured evidence and a packed jury—and the 'traitor's' head was exposed on London Bridge. In Canterbury lived More's favourite daughter, Margaret, who had married into a prominent Canterbury family, the Ropers, living in St. Dunstan's parish. According to tradition she secured the pathetic relic, and brought the head to Canterbury for reverent burial in the family vault in St. Dunstan's church. A tablet at the east end of the church commemorates this event, and as in the nineteenth century the Pope beatified Sir Thomas More, there are annual Roman Catholic pilgrimages to the tomb.

To even the account of death and torture, Henry's daughter, Bloody Mary, used a field in South Canterbury as a convenient spot for burning alive some of those who dared dissent from her religious beliefs. The name Martyrs' Field subsists to this day, and a stone cross and a garden are the memorial to these Protestant victims of intolerance.

In the reign of Henry's equally formidable but less bloodthirsty daughter Elizabeth, Canterbury again received the backwash of religious convulsions, this time of those of the Continent. The city is obviously a convenient place of refuge for persecuted European minorities, and during the religious wars of the sixteenth and seventeenth centuries in France and the Low Countries many hundreds of Walloons and Huguenots were allowed to settle in Canterbury. In the days of Queen Elizabeth a hundred families came to the city and more Huguenots flooded here after the revocation of the Edict of Nantes in 1685. It is said that at one time the Walloons and Huguenots, whose main occupation was weaving, had 2,000 looms in the city, a powerful and much-needed boost to the economy. The strangers were allowed to worship in St. Alphege's church and later in the crypt of the cathedral. In the nineteenth century when, by a mass emigration to Spitalfields and by natural absorption, the congregation had dwindled to a handful, their services were held in the Black Prince's Chantry, a small chapel leading from the crypt.

There is much Huguenot blood in Canterbury to this day. One of the main department stores in the city was, until a recent take-over 'Lefevres' (rhyming with 'receivers') and Charles Lefevre was the mayor who proved such a great leader in the tribulations of World War II. But Lefevre is not the only Canterbury name of French origin; Fedarb, Lepine, Delahaye and de Lassaux are some of the others.

England did not confine help to receiving refugees. Elizabeth, though at peace with Spain, was nevertheless conducting an unofficial war against her through 'volunteers'. In 1570 a formation, based at first on the London trained bands, was sent to help the Dutch in their fight for freedom. This company of soldiers was later to evolve into the Third Regiment of Foot, The Buffs, one of the oldest regiments of the British Army. From 1873, under the additional title of the Royal East Kent Regiment it had Canterbury as its home; the association with East Kent is mentioned in a royal warrant of 1782.

Basking in the prosperity that the Walloons brought, and in the prestige of Elizabeth's patronage, Canterbury had every reason to remember her reign with gratitude. The Queen secured the election as archbishop of Matthew Parker, a sound cleric, who rebuilt the Palace, spent time in Canterbury, and even wrote a letter which is still extant to the mayor reproving him for the desultory attendance by members of the Burghmote at the cathedral services.

The Queen showed her appreciation of the ancient city when she stayed in the King's House in the former St. Augustine's Abbey and held her court there for a fortnight in September 1573. To this reign also belongs the brief but brilliant career of Christopher Marlowe, probably Canterbury's most distinguished son. His father was a local shoemaker, always it seems in hot water of one kind or another, and the entry of Christopher's baptism is preserved in the register, now in the cathedral library, of the bombed church of St. George. Of Marlowe's plays and poems it was the assessment of Swinburne, that 'his faultless lyrics would have secured a place for him among the memorable men of his epoch even if his plays had perished with himself'; and of his plays that 'he first, and he alone, guided Shakespeare into the right way of work'. Kit Marlowe's life was pitifully short; at the age of twenty-nine he fell victim at Deptford to a tavern brawl connected, some think, with his work for the secret service.

Again and again the city was forced back on to religious dispute and its consequences. The Stuart kings leaned very heavily on the sect of the Church of England known as Puritans. Rather than be trammelled in their mode of worship and thought by the government of the day many of these enthusiastic religious rebels preferred exile, first in Holland and afterwards across the Atlantic in New England. The emigrants to Massachusetts have become legendary under the name of the Pilgrim Fathers, and it is with no little satisfaction that the citizens of Canterbury can claim two of this distinguished band as fellow townsmen, Robert Cushman and James Chiltern. Cushman, it is true, was not born in the city but he grew up there, being apprenticed to a grocer and tallow chandler. He became a freeman of the city but then quarrelled with the church authorities, refused to attend their services and finally left and went to Holland to join other Protestant exiles. In 1620 he wrote a letter from London to his fellow exiles at Leyden telling them that he had hired a ship, which although he did not name it, must, it is considered, have been the *Mayflower*. (One has to reject the theory of some historians that the Dutch themselves hired the ship, so anxious were they to be rid of this awkward squad.) Robert Cushman has descendants in the U.S.A. to this day. James Chiltern, as far as one knows, not only lived in Canterbury but was born there, and he was one of those who signed the Mayflower compact at Provincestown on the tip of Cape Cod before the final landing at Plymouth. We have already heard of Canterbury's claim to be the Mother of England; might she not also claim to be the midwife of Massachusetts?

Archivists are still hopeful of proving that as well as the Pilgrim Fathers, Franklin Roosevelt, James Madison and even Robert E. Lee had connections with Canterbury families of the sixteenth and seventeenth centuries. It would be ironical if one had to reflect, after the part played by Chiltern and Cushman, that the trouble that their descendants got into at Bull Run and Chancellorsville was organised by a Virginian whose family roots went back to the same ancient English city.

Of James I we need only say that he gave permission for the city to acquire a sword to be carried before the mayor, which it still is today, and will continue to be until the city is swallowed in the abyss. This particular weapon was, however, symbolic rather of what was to happen in the reign of James's son, Charles I, than of the uneventful days (so far as Canterbury was concerned) of James I. When Charles (who had spent his wedding night at St. Augustine's seventeen years' earlier) raised his standard at Nottingham in 1642 he was accepting the challenge of a civil war in which the part to be played by the county of Kent would be of no little significance. And what went on in Kent was often influenced by what took place in Canterbury.

In the early years of the war the city was plagued by the activities of a Puritan fanatic known as Blue Dick, alias Richard Culmer. After trying to make trouble for the harmless Walloons, Culmer started a violent dispute over the elections to what has come down in history as the Short Parliament. He objected to the archbishop having his secretary elected. Although Dean Bargrave was a Royalist, he was unable to line up the city and the county behind the King, and in fact as soon as a Cavalier coup was thought to be impending Parliament sent another destructive fanatic, Colonel Edwyn Sandys, to take possession of the cathedral, where the Dean and Chapter had been foolish enough to stock arms and gunpowder. The troops despoiled the interior of the cathedral, leaving behind in the city a legacy of bitterness and causing damage which cost £12,000, later on, to repair. A further minor revolt against Parliament caused a clamp-down on Royalist sympathisers; then Deans and Chapters were abolished, and this let in the crank Culmer, who ran amuck in the cathedral. Let Blue Dick tell his own story.

. . . 'Many window-images . . . were demolished . . .,' he says, 'many idols of stone, thirteen representing Christ and His twelve apostles . . . were all cast down headlong, and some fell on their heads and their mitres brake their neck . . . And then . . . the commissioners fell presently to work on the great Idolatrous window . . . (with) the picture of God the Father, and of Christ, . . . and the picture of the Holy Ghost in the form of a Dove, and of the 12 apostles; and . . . seven large pictures of the Virgin Mary, in seven glorious appearances, as of the angels lifting her into heaven, and the sun, moon, and stars under her feet . . . Their prime cathedral saint, Archbishop Thomas Becket, was most rarely pictured . . . with cope, rochet, mitre, crozier . . . Now it is more defaced than any window in that cathedral. Whilst judgement was executing on the idols in that window, the cathedralists cried out . . . Hold your hands, Holt, Holt, heer's Sir, etc. A minister (Culmer himself) being then on the top of the City ladder, near 60 steps high, with a whole pike in his hand rattling down proud Becket's glassy bones. . . . to him it was said 'tis a shame for a minister to be seen there . . . Some wished he might break his neck, others said it should cost blood...'

And so Culmer's account goes on, page after page; for the devastation lasted three days; and at the Restoration seventeen years later the reinstated Dean and Chapter found the cathedral in a 'sad, forlorn and languishing condition' and 'more like some ruined monastery than a church.' The miracle is that so much escaped—more indeed than in any other cathedral, except York Minster. Who can have the slightest sympathy with Master Culmer when his exploits resulted in a riot and threats to his life?

Historians divide the Civil War, or Great Rebellion, into two parts. After Naseby, Parliament seemed to have prevailed, but somehow fighting started up again in 1648. Kent was aflame and the conflagration was set off by a riot at Canterbury on Christmas Day 1647, which arose from the mayor's dutiful order that the market should be held, ignoring, as the Puritans ordained, the day of Christmas. Various cudgels were wielded and pates broken, the mayor knocked down and his cloak dirtied. Soon after, soldiers joined the rabble and brought with them two footballs. The ale houses were opened to all comers: 'Nothing to pay and welcome, gentlemen', while the wretched Culmer was chased round the city and pelted with mud. The Cavaliers asserted their authority, reduced this random rout to martial order, and made the city ready to stand a siege. When quiet had been restored, and the effects of so much free drink had worn off, the more moderate element asserted themselves and negotiated with both the Cavaliers and the Parliamentary forces, and in the end the rebels were forced to capitulate. The city gates of Canterbury were broken up and burnt, and stretches of the town wall were pulled down, never to be rebuilt.

A further rebellion in Kent resulted in the Parliamentary General Fairfax's advancing into the county and taking Maidstone by storm. Canterbury was again in the limelight as the place where the defeated remnants then concentrated, but when Fairfax approached, the city could not well be defended because of the gaps in the wall, and the lack of gates, so once again there was an ignominious surrender. When the country eventually got tired of the government of the Commonwealth, it was at

The great mass of the medieval Westgate
Aerial view of the city and cathedral

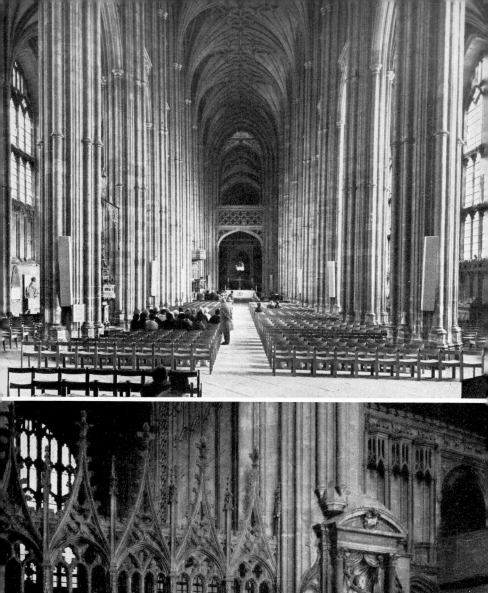

Canterbury again that Kent's declaration was published favouring constitutional monarchy, and when General Monk marched in from Scotland and put an end to the Commonwealth, it was there that Charles II spent the first night of his restored reign after landing from the Continent at Dover.

Canterbury's part in the Civil War was somewhat confused and ineffective because of a lack of agreement between the responsible establishment and the more volatile Cavalier element. However, the city certainly gave the Parliament men a great deal of trouble and caused them to recall an observation of 1642 that 'the Kentish men are a people that are sooner drawn by gentle means than in any way enforced. Their affection must flow uncompelled.'

So the King was on the throne, the Vicar of Bray was in his pulpit, the lawyers were using Latin again, and the restored archbishop, Juxon, who as Bishop of London had administered the last consolations to Charles I on the scaffold, gave back to the Christchurch Gateway the oaken doors which display his arms today. It was back to the good old days, and to celebrate them the Corporation, after a year or two, purchased a silver-gilt mace bearing Charles's initials and costing £62 10s. Under brother James, however, the citizens soon found out that the golden days of Charles were indeed over, when the former began to purge municipal corporations of his political opponents, especially Anglicans and Tories, a selection which denuded the Canterbury Corporation of most of its members, including the mayor. Within a year, however, the evicted were back in office, and the charter which had been taken away was restored. James had seen the danger of his high-handed policies, but too late to save his tottering throne; within months, with prodigious consumption of beef, tongues, ham, fowls, lobsters, oysters and anchovies, and many gallons of wine, the city was celebrating the proclamation of King William and Queen Mary.

The nave of the cathedral
The north-west transept, where Becket was murdered

JOHN TWYNE

IN an age in which Nicholas Wotton could be both Dean of Canterbury and Dean of York, and at the same time a politician and diplomatist going on embassies and errands abroad, it is scarcely surprising to hear that the first headmaster of the King's School, John Twyne, held, beside his scholastic appointment, the offices of alderman, sheriff, Member of Parliament and mayor of Canterbury.

The careers of the two men were, however, in other respects dissimilar. While Wotton was able to continue untroubled in his offices through the reigns of Henry VIII, Edward VI, Mary and Elizabeth, Twyne, having managed to survive one enforced visit to the Tower of London in 1553 was eventually hounded out of his various offices by the Archbishop of Canterbury with a stern admonition to go easy on the bottle.

John Twyne had a considerable reputation; as a schoolmaster whose pupils benefited greatly from his training; as an antiquary who de-bunked Geoffrey of Monmouth and his romantic tales of a Canterbury founded by Brutus from Troy; and as a scholar who wrote copiously in the Latin tongue on religious and political subjects. After graduating B.C.L. at Oxford, John married. He then became master of the free school at Canterbury, a school 'much frequented by the youth of the neighbourhood'. This was in the good old days before the dissolution of the monastery, and the establishment was the one appearing in the records as the Archbishop's School.

Most of Twyne's literary works have perished, but a book in two volumes *De Rebus Albionicis, Britannicis atque Angliis*, which he wrote for his son Thomas, the latter published after his father's death.

The dissolution of the monasteries must have been a blow to John Twyne, who had little enough of Wotton's flexibility, and was friendly with the priors of both Christchurch and St. Augustine's, and with many of the monks. He was perhaps lucky, in view of his religious convictions, to be appointed in 1542 the first headmaster of the newly-constituted King's School. He was already prosperous and had bought property in Canterbury; he now found it possible to become active in municipal affairs, and in 1544 he was sheriff, and in 1553 an alderman. That year was his *annus mirabilis*; in January he represented the city in Parliament, but by May, having given offence to the Duke of Northumberland, the protestant political boss, Twyne sampled the hospitality of the Tower. He was eventually let out, and promptly re-elected M.P. and also mayor. By this time Edward VI had died, and after the episode of Lady Jane Grey Mary Tudor succeeded.

A rebellion immediately broke out in Kent, and Sir Thomas Wyat seized Rochester and was soon winning adherents. But John Twyne would have none of this; history tells us that he actively opposed the insurgents. The Corporation minutes record that a person was paid 5s. to ride to Maidstone, to know the state of the commotion begun there by Wyat and his accomplices; labourers were employed to fetch guns and other ammunition from the archbishop's palace for the city's defence. (What the ammunition was doing at the palace we are not told.) There was a whip-round for contributions for the repair of the city walls, which raised £42 7s. 5½d. After Wyat had come to his inevitable end on the scaffold, Queen Mary sent thanks to the mayor and citizens for their fidelity, and four years later the queen came to the city to renew her thanks.

John Twyne was now at the height of his fortune. But his felicity was short-lived. Within two years of Mary's death in 1558 an ecclesiastical visitation to Canterbury ordered him to 'abstain from ryot and drunkenness and not to intermeddle with any public office in the town'. Within a year he lost his post as headmaster of the school; Archbishop Parker was now on his track and managed to edge him out of a comfortable little sinecure that he held in the village of Littlebourne—keepership of the Forest of Rivingwood. However, John retained his aldermanry, possibly because it was as much a proprietory right as an administrative position, and his religious ideas did not stand in the way of a quiet life as rector of the village of Preston. In this he was at least luckier than his predecessor, Nicholas Faunt.

John Twyne will long be remembered in Canterbury for the highly quotable words that he wrote in praise of the city, which are so proudly displayed at the Beaney Institute. He will long be remembered at the King's School not only as its first headmaster but even more as the cornerstone on which the theory of the great antiquity of the school is built. Some enthusiasts assert boldly that the school was founded in A.D. 600; more cautious claimants say that, with gaps, it goes back to the time of St. Augustine; others unkindly point out that some of these gaps are many centuries in length. Most of the facts we already know—the dissolution of the monastery of Christ Church and the endowment made by the king for fifty poor scholars out of part of the revenues which he thus seized; the name, on that account of the King's School. Several schools claim an earlier date for their foundation than 1541; how far they can go in proving these claims is another matter.

It is round our friend John Twyne that the argument centres; because he was the last headmaster of the Archbishop's School, and the first of the King's School, some scholars argue that the latter is only a continuation of the former, and as they do not know exactly when the Archbishop's School was started assume (it is safe they say to do this) that there would be such a school when the monastery was founded by St. Augustine, nearly fourteen centuries ago.

It seems that the first mention of the Archbishop's School, as such, is in an appeal to the Pope in the year 1259. An Old Langtonian might point out that by hitching the history of his school to that of a predecessor, he can take its story back to 1224, when the journal of Thomas Eccleston, the Franciscan, has a well-known passage about the friars using a boys' school at the Poor Priests' Hospital, where later the Bluecoat was to be transformed into the Simon Langton School. The argument could go on for ever without result. The best answer is that given by an O.K.S. who wrote one of the most recent histories of the school. Suggesting that there can be no question of a school being established in St. Augustine's time, he observes that education was merely one of the functions of a cathedral, and once the matter is seen in this light the controversy disappears. Canterbury has the oldest great church; therefore Canterbury has the oldest education, observes Mr. D. L. Edwards.

What more can be said?

SEVEN

SWINGS AND ROUNDABOUT

THE years between the arrival in England of William of Orange and the outbreak of Hitler's War represent a quarter of a millennium of time, but one looks in vain for great events in any way comparable to those of the previous 250 years. Perhaps this was a happy time in Canterbury—that is the usual conclusion that people draw from the absence of history—perhaps the excitements of the Tudor and Stuart eras had exhausted everyone so much that they needed a long rest; it is difficult to say. We know only that if great events fail to happen the chronicler cannot record them; and has to make do with such small ones as he can find. These may, however, like specks of matter swimming in deep water, show the direction of the current of history.

To begin with, in the late seventeenth and early eighteenth centuries, Canterbury's importance was perhaps flatteringly emphasised by an impressive number of royal visits; they were probably due less to the prestige of the city than to the geography of Kent. The direct route to the Continent was the London–Canterbury–Dover road, and as Charles II had found on an historic occasion, the city is just the right distance from Dover to be what the French call a *ville d'étape*, or as the modern Caravan Club unflatteringly terms it, a 'night halt'.

No doubt the recently-formed connection, first with Holland and later with Hanover, would stimulate the royal enthusiasm for Continental travel. But it is only fair to recall that people as important as the younger Pitt, and the Prince Regent himself, managed to find the time to accept the gift of the Freedom of the City, and to come here for the attendant ceremonies and junketing.

Ordinary life went on; at irregular intervals murderers and other felons were publicly hanged, first at Oaten Hill, and later in front of the Westgate. For the more frequent entertainment of the not-too-sensitive, the lesser and more numerous criminal fry were exposed to punishments only one degree less ferocious. For trying to worm his way into the sacred (and profit earning) ranks of the Freemen by trickery, a rogue is put in the pillory (I should just think so); for stealing articles of trifling value, a woman is whipped in the Cornmarket; for more serious thefts one man is burnt on the hand in open court by the gaoler at Sessions, and another taken to the market-place, stripped to the waist and flogged until he bleeds. And this sort of thing did not go out with full-bottomed wigs; it continued right through the polite and polished eighteenth century.

But, all the time, the stream of history was flowing silently and unfavourably for Canterbury. When John Bird Sumner was enthroned as archbishop in the cathedral in 1848, he was the first primate to have taken the trouble to come to the city for that purpose for over 130 years. The archbishops during that time, and for long after, had no palace or other residence in the city; Archbishop Parker's building had long since been removed. It really was beginning to look as if the destruction of Becket's shrine and the cessation of the pilgrimages were at last beginning to have their effect, and that Canterbury was degenerating, if it had not already degenerated, into a mere backwater. But we should not be too hard on the archbishops; their concentration on their job at Lambeth (as long as they *were* concentrating on it) was the logical conclusion of the decision of Lanfranc to think of the church first, and Canterbury local affairs second; the pressures towards centralisation that were affecting other walks of life would be bearing upon the church too, and the journey to Canterbury before the age of steam was too long to be undertaken without good reason. It is something more than a coincidence that as soon as there was a railway between London and Canterbury the primates quickly began to take, or at any rate to show, more interest in their metropolitical city. In this as in other respects the age of steam was definitely a 'Good Thing' for Canterbury. And a 'Good Thing' for Their Graces, too.

In the seventeenth century Canterbury was among the most populous places in England; by 1939 it was far down the list. Defoe says of it, in the eighteenth century: '. . . its antiquity seems to be its greatest beauty; the houses are truly ancient, and the many ruins of churches, chapels, oratories, and smaller cells of religious people, makes the place look like a general ruin a little recovered.' The 'truly ancient' houses of Defoe are even more ancient today. It is a solemn reflection that the old half-timbered places that people still live in today, Wealden houses, some architects call them, were already three hundred if not four hundred years old in Defoe's time. St. Radigund's House and 44 Ivy Lane are good examples; The Chequer of the Hope, The Falstaff Inn and All Saints' Court in All Saints' Lane, less old by a century, could still have been amongst those that attracted the writer's attention. Others that he could have noticed may now have perished, but lovers of antiquity, exploring the old lanes and alleys, will be surprised to find how many have not. No. 16 Watling Street, one of the city's most notable buildings, was a mere eighty or so years of age when Defoe was looking round; it was built in the year that Charles I came to St. Augustine's for his wedding night, 1625.

Defoe continues: 'The city will scarce bear being called populous, were it not for two or three thousand French Protestants, which, including men, women and children, they say there are in it, and yet they tell me the number of these decrease daily.'

He had also heard of the efforts to make the Stour navigable, but even in his time the project had been abandoned, and the locks and sluices were run to decay. By way of compensation he noted that there was at Canterbury the greatest plantation of hops in the whole island. 'The great wealth and increase of the City' was from this almost incredible area of 6,000 acres, within a few miles, planted with hops.

Some years before Defoe's visit to the city when he was so surprised to discover the extent of the hop gardens, he had interested himself in a Canterbury affair even more incredible, that of Mrs. Veal's Apparition, and had published a pamphlet about it that has become well known. Its title is a very long one: *A True Relation of the Apparition of one Mrs. Veal, the next day after her death, to one Mrs. Bargrave, at Canterbury, the 8th September, 1705. Which Apparition recommends the Perusal of Drelincourt's Book of Consolations against the Fears of Death.* But there is this to be said for it; however much you may read about Mrs. Veal and Mrs. Bargrave and their various friends and relations, you will not get much further than what is said in the title of Defoe's tract. The malicious suggestion is made that his effusion was really a 'commercial' for Drelincourt's book, to which in fact it was printed as a preface. This indeed was the view of Sir Walter Scott, who spoke of 'summoning up a ghost from the grave to bear witness in favour of a halting body of divinity'. Those who are loath to let slip a good thing when they have it answer Sir Walter with circumstantial proof that Mrs. Veal and Mrs. Bargrave were real persons—about as convincing as the inn-keeper in *Barnaby Rudge*; when people doubted the tale that Queen Elizabeth had slept there, he pointed out that the mounting-block on which she was supposed to have stood was a real mounting-block.

The facts, such as they are, are very brief. On Saturday, the 8th September, 1705, Mrs. Veal of Dover visited her friend Mrs. Bargrave at her house in Canterbury. Nothing very remarkable about that one would think, until told that in fact Mrs. Veal had died at Dover the previous day, Friday, a good twenty-four hours before she called on her friend at Canterbury. Some importance is attached to the fact that a letter was written within five days of the supposed occurrence describing it in circumstantial detail; the author was a person signing himself, or herself, 'E.B.' and the recipient is known to history only as 'Dear Madam'.

The affair soon acquired an aura of respectability and a snobbish cachet from the display of interest by persons of quality. There was a man in Canterbury, Stephen Gray, a dyer by profession, who was interested also in astronomy and used to take observations for the Astronomer Royal, at that time John Flamsteed, at Greenwich. It seems that Prince George of Denmark, Queen Anne's consort, heard about Mrs. Veal and her Apparition, and Flamsteed obligingly agreed to write to his Canterbury correspondent to get the details; Gray replied with a lengthy report covering much of the same ground as 'E.B.' with a lot more about the character and background of Mrs. Bargrave and her husband.

The essentials, however, are soon told; Mrs. Veal, having appeared, told her Canterbury friend that she was about to go on a long journey, and she wished Mrs. Bargrave to arrange with her (Mrs. Veal's) brother to have a tombstone made for their *mother's* grave, but large enough to take Mrs. Veal's name as well. At the same time, the visitor expressed the glowing commendation of Drelincourt's book which so aroused the suspicions of the more sceptical. For what it is worth, Mrs. Veal then said she would like to see Mrs. Bargrave's young daughter who was for

The Great Cloister and chapter house with Bell Harry beyond

some reason away from the house. The mother went to find her child, but no sooner was she out of the front door than Mrs. Veal also left the house, saying she was going to see a cousin of hers in the city. But neither the cousin, nor Mrs. Bargrave, nor anyone else, ever clapped eyes on Mrs. Bargrave's caller from that moment onward. There is an account of the affair in a contemporary newspaper now in the New York Public Library, and the intermittent stream of articles about it in learned journals and elsewhere shows no sign of drying up.

By the early nineteenth century a scandalous state of nepotism and plurality obtained at the cathedral. In the time of Archbishop Manners-Sutton, if we are to believe what we are told (not by the enemies of the church but by its own historians), rectories, vicarages, and chapelries, beside preacherships and dignities in cathedrals, were shared out wholesale amongst the members of the primate's family. Any relation of his who had less than three or four well-paid sinecures in addition to his normal job considered himself hardly done by. The Dean of Canterbury married one of His Grace's daughters, and struck it rich to the tune of £10,000 a year in valuable preferments; with income tax nominal, and money worth perhaps ten times its present value, it seems an ungallant reflection on the attractions of Miss Manners-Sutton that such a stupendous dowry was needed to get her off Papa's hands. Her sister's ecclesiastical boy-friend did as well, if not better; no figures are given, but while holding the Archdeaconry of Canterbury, James Croft also enjoyed *in commendam*, that is to say without doing a stroke of work, 'the rich livings of Cliffe-at-Hoo and Saltwood, as well as the curacy of Hythe'. No doubt to stop their tongues from wagging, the other members of the chapter who had not the good fortune to be related to His Grace held, in addition to their stalls, livings in various distant parts of Kent, and even in London, which they must have regarded as sources of revenue and nothing more.

This being the way in which ecclesiastical appointments were distributed, we are not surprised to learn that from time to time the Dean and Chapter displayed poor taste and general stupidity in carrying out their duty of looking after the fabric of the cathedral. Professor Willis rightly contrasts the periods of reverent care and improvement of the monastery during the Middle Ages, with the neglect, destruction and cupidity of the

8

Tomb of the Black Prince in Trinity Chapel

Reformation and the Rebellion, and the meddlesome ignorance and indifference of these times.

Until the eighteenth century the nave of Canterbury Cathedral had many ledger stones, flat gravestones ornamented with the funeral brasses of many of the old priors. Although the nave was not used at all at this time, the Dean and Chapter, thinking that they were acting as persons of good taste, completely refloored it in Portland stone and removed all the interesting tombstones and brasses. They also whitewashed—'daubed' as their critics say— every piece of the cathedral where an old wall-painting or other decoration remained from ancient times and completely destroyed these interesting survivals.

From about 1800, until the Christchurch Gateway was restored in the 1930s by the Friends of Canterbury Cathedral it stood shorn of its turrets by the cathedral surveyor, merely because the man he was speaking to, Alderman Simmons, had remarked that the turrets prevented him from checking his watch against the cathedral clock when sitting in his office in the High Street. 'Can't you pull them down,' asked the alderman. 'It shall be done,' replied Jesse White, who trotted off to tell the Dean that the turrets were insecure and too heavy for the gateway. They were then removed. Until the Friends stepped in to carry through what must surely rank as one of their finest achievements, the edifice was in a sadly dilapidated state. The elaborately carved and panelled Caen stone had rotted away in the long years since 1507 when the work was finished, but now that it has been restored we can see that its style was not unjustly compared with that of Henry VII's Chapel at Westminster which was built about the same time.

In 1832 the chapter discovered in an old book what is described as 'tittle-tattle' to the effect that when Henry IV's coffin was being brought by sea to Faversham before burial in the cathedral, a storm blew and the sailors decided to lighten ship by throwing the corpse overboard. The historically-minded chapter convinced themselves that the whole polite and learned world must be agog to ascertain the truth or otherwise of this story, and on this pretext they pried into the tomb, cut open the leaden case within, and were able to reassure an expectant country—yes, the king was there all right. But it is nice to be quite sure, isn't it?

In the reign of George II Archbishop Herring had proved himself equal to the difficult feat of outdoing even the Dean and

Chapter in philistinism; the Primate had heard that the King of
Sardinia would like to have the relics of Saint Anselm. This
would doubtless be because Aosta, the birthplace of Anselm, was
part of the king's dominions. The general attitude of the archbishop was dig them up, wrap them up in a parcel and send
them to the king, if that would satisfy him. And if this was
impossible, 'he would make a conscience of palming on the
simpleton any old bishop with the name of Anselm'. The sharp
reply from the Dean and Chapter was that the shrine of Anselm,
like that of Becket and Dunstan, had been destroyed at the
Reformation, and that if they were to dig up any bones no doubt
the King of Sardinia or his representative would have to come
along, and the state of the crypt of the cathedral was so neglected
that 'it would not be desirable to have a foreign personage of high
character to take offence at the manner of our using it.'

Perhaps the lowest point in Canterbury's history was reached in
1832 when Archbishop Howley made himself so unpopular with
the citizens by opposing the Reform Bill that they treated him as
their ancestors had treated the obnoxious Blue Dick; they pelted
him with offensive missiles, not excluding dead cats.

However, even at this low ebb in the prestige of those attached
to the cathedral there had been a brighter and more colourful
episode to cheer people up a little. Not everyone knows that
Lord Nelson lived for many years in the precincts of Canterbury
Cathedral and was there visited by Lady Hamilton. Surely this
cannot be true? Well, it was not *the* Lord Nelson, but his brother
and heir, Dr. William Nelson, alias The Right Hon. and Rev.
Earl Nelson, D.D., who was a canon from 1803 to 1838, and used
to take a newspaper into the services in case they should prove too
boring. After Horatio's death, Lady Hamilton used to visit his
brother and sister-in-law, but the Canterbury ladies, except for a
Mrs. Bridges, refused to meet Emma socially. The broadminded
Mrs. Bridges and Nelson's erstwhile inamorata regaled a congregation in the cathedral by singing together the anthem *My
song shall be of mercy and judgment*. When Lady Hamilton offered
to sing a further anthem in aid of the County Hospital, Dean
Powys had to pretend that he was deaf so that he should not have
either to accept or to decline, and the second anthem was not sung.

Of this Dean it was said *to his credit* that he always came to
Canterbury during Lent.

Neglected and spurned by its archbishops and indifferently

served by its deans, the city was also slipping back in secular importance. In the early nineteenth century it was still the largest town in Kent but it did not benefit, as it did not suffer, from the industrial revolution. In the new Britain, with a rapidly growing population and expanding towns, it was a case of running very fast to keep in the same relative place, and Canterbury was scarcely running at all.

The church, however, was now putting its house in order. We have heard of the Reformation, and some of the actions of the reformers lead us to question whether 'reformation' is an adequate or proper description of what they got up to, but no name has been assigned to the no less fundamental change that Canterbury witnessed in the high officials of the church from about the middle of the nineteenth century. Perhaps the better communications which had enabled the archbishops to show a more proper regard for their own cathedral enabled them also to take a greater part in Canterbury life. Whatever the reason, it was a great day for the city when Archbishop Frederick Temple decided to rebuild the palace and make a home for himself in Canterbury.

In 1836 the Ecclesiastical Commissioners had been set up by Act of Parliament, and these unsympathetic spoil-sports put a stop to the cosy little game of Happy Families that its critics called pluralities and nepotism. At Canterbury they went further, and reduced the number of prebendaries (what are now called canons) from twelve to six. This halving of the numbers of the sect who, according to Archbishop Cranmer, 'spent their time in much idleness, and their substance in superfluous belly cheer' had an interesting side-effect; the now superfluous houses at the east end of the cathedral were pulled down and their removal exposed to view the arches of the Norman infirmary which had been built into their fabric.

Furthermore, having to work with the Ecclesiastical Commissioners and their architects had a restraining effect on the vagaries of the Dean and Chapter. This perhaps might have proved unnecessary, because by the 1850s the cathedral seems to have seen the last of the worthy but somewhat odd-ball type of eccentric who provides such excellent reading to the student of the eighteenth and early nineteenth centuries. Since the 1850s Canterbury has been, on the whole, very lucky with its deans, who have included Farrar, author of *Eric, or Little by Little*; Bell, founder of the Friends of the Cathedral, and Sheppard, and more recent well-known characters whom it is perhaps a little early, and a little invidious, to assess.

After the self-cleansing by the church from its abuses, the name of Canterbury had become almost literally one to conjure with throughout the world; the Lambeth Conference recognised Canterbury Cathedral as its spiritual meeting-place; and the thousands of ordinary people coming from far afield to see the cathedral were being spoken of again as pilgrims.

So everything in the Anglican garden was lovely; but there were plenty of Canterbury citizens who were not Anglicans, and the spectacle that the Church of England presented in the eighteenth and early nineteenth centuries can scarcely have discouraged the growth of the infinite variety of Baptists, General and Particular, Unitarians, Wesleyans, Prebyterians, Congregationalists and Quakers whose communities the city nurtured.

The stories of both the Baptists and the Presbyterians are complex and puzzling for the simple reason that the practice of dissent is not by any manner of means confined to one occasion; the existence of a duly organised congregation of Dissenters enabled the dedicated dissenter (with a small 'd') to dissent from *that*. A good deal of time seems to have been taken by the Baptists, in particular, in dealing with the alleged backsliding of fellow Baptists of the congregation, while every now and then it would be discovered that the brethren had slipped so far that they had turned themselves into some different kind of animal altogether. To change the metaphor, the poorer congregations seem to have been rather like hermit crabs, using other people's discarded accommodation, particularly friaries, Black and Grey. It was a group of Baptists at the Blackfriars that drifted into Unitarianism, while a strictly Calvinistic band of *Particular* Baptists ensconced themselves in the snug little Zoar Chapel built into a bastion of the city wall in Lower Bridge Street, and in the eighteenth century the Greyfriars was the meeting place of Presbyterians. Both Baptists and Presbyterians had been around in Canterbury for many years, from the seventeenth century in fact, while, until it was completely destroyed in the blitz, the Society of Friends boasted of owning the oldest nonconformist meeting house in the city, to which William Penn, founder of Pennsylvania, had contributed. It is sad to read that these harmless people had their martyrs; nine of them died in prison in Canterbury, in Good King Charles' Golden Days. But even Dissent seems to be on the retreat before the advance of Indifference. Some years ago the large and impressive Congregationalist Church in Guildhall Street became redundant and was taken into Lefevre's furniture department, while the prominently sited Presbyterian Church—a landmark for the Continental travellers on Rheims Way—whose spire silhouetted against the westering sun Canterbury has admired for years, that too some twenty years later suffered the same fate, and by the time these words are read will have made way for an office block.

A congregation of Baptists now flourishes in its own church in St. George's Place, while the Wesleyan Methodists, founded by the master himself in 1750, have an elegantly modelled church, dated 1811, set back from St. Peter's Street, and the Congregational/Presbyterian rearguard are concentrated in Watling Street. In Burgate—designed, as was the Presbyterian church, by the indefatigable J. G. Hall, and dedicated by Cardinal Manning in the 1870s—is the Roman Catholic church of St. Thomas of Canterbury.

The oecumenical spirit, it is pleasing to report, is strong in present-day Canterbury, and the existence of different denominations gives variety rather than dissension to the spiritual community.

Meanwhile, what had been happening to the city? Although its efforts to run with its industrialised rivals had left it well down the course, it would be wrong to think that there had been no activity. Perhaps it would be better in some directions if there had been none at all, as 'progress' in the latter part of the eighteenth century seems to have consisted largely in taking down various ancient gates, arches and other buildings; the old Watergate by Abbot's Mill in 1769; the buildings over Wincheap Gate the next year; Burgate (partially) and Ridingate 1781 and 1782, the Roman arch of Worthgate in 1791, and St. George's Gate in 1802. Northgate was 'widened' in 1787; whether this involved the destruction of the old gate, which had St. Mary Northgate's Church over it, is not clear; if it did manage to survive the widening (the church was supported on massive wooden piers) it was not for long; by the early years of the nineteenth century it was a case of 'gone for ever'. This holocaust left only the Westgate, and a new Ridingate, paid for by the generous Alderman Simmons, still standing.

It was only in 1787 that a Local Act was passed for paving, watching and lighting the city under the direction of Improvement Commissioners. Unless you understand the limited functions of the medieval municipal corporations, it seems incredible that these commissioners were necessary. What was the old Corporation doing? Was there no watching, etc., before 1787? The answer is, yes; but on a crude sort of basis of 'take-it-in-turns, or else face a fine of a shilling', rather like fire-watching in the last war, only in all probability less efficient. There was some attempt at paving the streets—by making every householder look after the bit of highway in front of his house. The Corporation's basic functions, as stated by old Alderman Bunce round about 1800, were of the simplest, namely, admitting freemen, appointing city officers, regulating trade, managing the city's estates, and generally looking after the rights and privileges of the city and its citizens. But the Corporation had the power, if it wanted, as a chartered body, to do anything that a 'natural person', as the lawyers put it, could do. Thus it superintended the city's water supply, such as it was, contributed to the cost of building the old Kent and Canterbury Hospital, and even purchased a fire-engine for the citizens to use. And it must have been a jolly good fire-engine too; it cost all of £52 8s.

Then again, in a glow of patriotism, in 1798, the Corporation gave the Government £300 towards the cost of fighting the French (on top of a hundred guineas already voted for the volunteers) and promised £200 a year for the duration of the war. (This was a logical development of what went on in medieval times, before the government had the defence of the country organised, when the Corporation had actually raised, paid, and clothed their own soldiers. And very dressy they must have been, with the city paying for them to have red crosses on their green tunics). In any case the war proved to be good for trade when, in the closing years of the century, first cavalry and then infantry barracks were built in Northgate. But the benefit was short-lived; once Boney was beat, the city began to lament the departure of the soldiery. Wars and crises have since come and gone, and the military population has fluctuated correspondingly. It is now (in the 1970s) at a low ebb, but the city has succeeded in prising only a small part of the huge sterilised area from the grip of the military authorities.

Guildhall Street, which they constructed, is a visible relic from the days of the Improvement Commissioners; the absence of porticoes and steps in front of many of the older buildings is an invisible one, for the Commisioners went through the city like a ruthless juggernaut, erasing without mercy everything that in any way impeded the highway. In the course of the nineteenth century their functions were taken over by the reformed Corporation, which incidentally was shorn of the old 'liberties' in Nackington, Littlebourne and other wild rural areas, but received in highly beneficial exchange, full sway over the cathedral precincts, the Manors of Longport and Westgate, the 'borough' of Staplegate, and any other Passport-to-Pimlico enclaves still left over from the medieval chaos.

A strange, out-of-character, episode is the opening of the Canterbury–Whitstable Railway in 1830. At a time when people were complaining that the town had 'gone down, in point of wealth', when its only manufacturing industry, the weaving of silk and cotton had, after years of ups and downs, finally packed up, it took unusual boldness to pioneer this new form of transport; pioneer is the right word for this was amongst the first ten passenger railways in the whole world. Over the hilly part of the track, at the Canterbury end, the carriages were hauled by cable, operated by stationary engines, but on the flat ground near Whitstable traction was by locomotive. The Invicta (for such was its name), was built at Newcastle by Robert Stephenson, the seventieth in the world. But there was little reward for the Canterbury Railroad Company's directors and shareholders. It was sixteen years before a dividend was paid—of two per cent, a figure not likely to cause inflation in the Canterbury commercial world; the Invicta did not work very well and was taken out of service. The unexplained decision, or oversight, by which the Invicta has survived is perhaps the most noteworthy action or inaction of the old Rail Road Company and of the South Eastern Railway to whom they handed over. Some people are never satisfied unless they can claim some specific record or first-ever achievement. Well, here it is—the first railway-passenger season ticket in the whole history of the human race was issued by the Canterbury Rail Road Company.

And though the railway itself was finally dismantled in the 1950s the Invicta can be seen in the Dane John Gardens to this very day.

After the Reform Act, the Canterbury pot simmered gently for the term of a century. Almost exactly at half-term came the one really important event; in 1888, when county and county borough councils were invented, the city in spite of its small size was given the valuable privilege of county borough status. This advantage it owed to the House of Lords, for the government of the day had not intended any such thing, and learnt the hard way that the name of Canterbury was still not to be trifled with.

By 1939 the population was static at about 24,000, having taken a century to reach that figure from the 16,000 of 1831. The modest growth in numbers, and perhaps higher standards, had spread houses and streets where fields had been before, first in the angle between St. Peter's Street and the old Greyfriars domain, then, almost contemporaneously, in Wincheap and North Holmes, St. Dunstan's and South Canterbury. The inter-war semi-detached culture flourished in St. Stephen's, near the Whitstable Road and the New and Old Dover Roads. The Old Dover Road was the most sought-after for the superior type of house occupied by what would now be termed executives.

There was still no manufacturing industry, except for one tannery and a few minor bits and pieces; the Walloons had all gone or been absorbed; two or three breweries had risen and died. With the building of one brand-new school and a few hundred municipal houses, local government was just beginning to stir after many years of slumber. Cars and buses were already bringing a healthy amount of new trade to supplement the old market-town activities, tourism was flourishing and Cricket Week was at its zenith. Happy, sleepy, Canterbury was the verdict of at least one observant traveller. H. V. Morton, in search of somewhere—Kent, England, Britain, no matter—saw air-raid warden equipment in the window of the A.R.P. headquarters in St. Margaret's Street. 'Surely,' smiled Mr. Morton indulgently, 'war will never come to Canterbury!'

But it did.

INTERLUDE

FRANCIS BENNETT-GOLDNEY

BETWEEN 1905 and 1918 Francis Bennett-Goldney filled at least three of the offices that John Twyne had held 350 years earlier; those of mayor, alderman and Member of Parliament for the city. In all other respects it would be difficult to imagine two careers in the same approximate walk of life more diverse in character, aims and achievement than those of Twyne and Goldney. As Francis was also Honorary Curator of the City Museum and a Fellow of the Society of Antiquaries, it might be thought that here was another parallel between their lives and interests. But Francis used his real or pretended knowledge of archaeology to further his civic ambitions rather than to spread enlightenment, and while John had gained credit by exploding an untrue legend about the origin of the city, Francis thought it was clever to foist on the public a new fiction about the Westgate.

Until he was twenty-seven, Francis went under the family name of Evans. Of Welsh stock long resident in the English Midlands, he had as uncle Sir John Evans—the author of the definitive work on the coins of the Ancient Britons, treasurer of the Royal Society, president of the Society of Antiquaries and a trustee of the British Museum—and as cousin Sir Arthur Evans, the celebrated archaeologist who excavated the palace of Knossos. Francis was left a fortune on condition that he adopted the surname 'Bennett-Goldney'. Goldney was his mother's maiden name, and we may presume that the testator was a member or connection of her family.

Why the scion of a distinguished Welsh family, born in Birmingham, educated at Bournemouth and Paris, and with a commission in the Middlesex militia should seek to make a public career in the City of Canterbury, history does not relate. However, armed with his double-barrelled name and the extensive fortune that went with it, he moved to Kent. A bachelor to the end, he lived with his mother. (Where his father was we are not told.) It is maliciously related that he was never averse to leaving mother when he wanted to make one of his little trips to Paris. After some years residence in the county he sought municipal honours at Canterbury; with his impressive presence, native cunning and a large collection of Roman, Saxon and other relics which he was prepared to loan *gratis*, he obtained for himself the twin honours of membership of the city council and honorary directorship of the Beaney Institute and Museum which were then being built. It required but three years from first election to the council to the mayoral chair, and only a little longer to an aldermanic robe. Having once secured the mayoralty, this new Augustus obtained each year from his brother councillors a renewal of his authority until the year 1910, when ambition began to nudge Frank to try for higher things. He learnt that the sitting Conservative Member of Parliament was not seeking re-election, and hastened to put himself forward to supply the vacancy. The immediate effect of this offer was to cause the sitting member to reconsider his decision, and stand after all. Goldney decided to fight the election himself as an Independent Unionist, and in a savage contest the sitting member narrowly retained the seat. But when within months another general election followed— those were the days of the crisis about the Parliament Act— Henniker Heaton's seconds were unable to get their candidate into shape for another round. A substitute had to be found, who proved no match for the up-and-coming Frank, and the latter was duly elected and retained the seat from 1910 until his death.

The Great War brought further opportunities for service to Goldney. He had leased a house in Barton Fields known by the prosaic name of Westfield House but re-christened by him more evocatively Abbot's Barton, and (all credit to him) he placed this house at the nation's disposal for use as a hospital. He also took on the duties of principal organiser of ambulance services in Kent.

In 1917 he was appointed honorary military attaché at the British Embassy in Paris. However, the year before he had been injured in a motor accident, and in July 1918 the injuries flared up and brought about his death in the American hospital at Brest.

Such in outline was the career of Francis Bennett-Goldney, pillar of respectability, Member of Parliament, and albeit in a limited sphere, honoured representative of His Britannic Majesty's Government.

Yet this was the man who purloined many of the city's precious documents, secured a sinecure employment for at least one favourite, and posed as the generous lender to the city of property that did not belong to him; in addition he became involved in one of the greatest scandals of Edwardian society, the disappearance of the Crown Jewels—of Ireland—and yet survived without noticeable damage to his municipal career or later parliamentary aspirations.

In May 1907 Goldney, when he was Mayor of Canterbury, obtained the unlikely appointment of Athlone Pursuivant of Arms in Ireland. Within two months of this appointment the Crown Jewels of Ireland, for the custody and safe-keeping of which the Office of Arms of Ireland was responsible, disappeared, and they have never been seen again from that day to this. While it was not suggested that Bennett-Goldney was criminally answerable for the disappearance, the fact is that at the desire of King Edward VII, Goldney and a number of his colleagues in the Office of Arms were requested to resign, a request with which Frank complied with alacrity.

Rumour suggests that the real purpose for which Goldney and his colleagues were required to sacrifice their heraldic careers was the prevention of the washing in public of a good deal of very dirty linen belonging to very, very eminent people.

Goldney, in fact, seemed to see in the affair a chance to increase his fame. He chose to regard his resignation as a form of martyrdom, and wrote a letter to *The Times* on the subject. He tried to intrigue with Sir Arthur Vicars, Ulster King of Arms, the man ultimately responsible for the security of the jewels, against Francis Shackleton (a brother of the explorer), whom Goldney strongly suspected of knowing more than he was prepared to tell about the disappearance of the jewels. Goldney was in and out of Scotland Yard in his efforts to implicate Shackleton. He invested the whole proceedings with a cloak and dagger atmosphere; the dagger was merely metaphorical, but the cloak part was literally true, as Goldney's accustomed attire in Canterbury was a black one with a scarlet lining. There is a suggestion that both Vicars and Shackleton were financially embarrassed, and sought Goldney's help. Did they really admit Goldney to their charmed circle with a view to sponging on him?

There is a highly mysterious sideline to the story of the Irish jewels; according to the well-known Canterbury character Mr.

J. G. B. Stone, another item that disappeared from Dublin Castle at the time the jewels were taken was the blue Garter that had belonged to the Duke of Marlborough. The sharp eye of Mr. Stone noticed that a similar Garter made its appearance on display at the Beaney Institute museum about this time, and on his drawing attention to it, suddenly it was withdrawn 'but by whom, when or how was never known'.

After the premature decease of Bennett-Goldney, the Corporation of Canterbury had the melancholy duty of suing the executors of their former mayor for the return of the many charters and civic documents that had somehow found their way into his effects, and were being offered for sale by auctioneers. Under threat of legal action, a picture loaned to the museum by Bennett-Goldney was returned to its owner, the Duke of Bedford. The whole affair reeks of intrigue and mystery.

One of Bennett-Goldney's distinctions is that of having deliberately invented and committed to print the fable, not very creditable to the city of his adoption, that it was only by the casting vote of the mayor that the Westgate was not pulled down in 1850 to enable Mr. Wombwell's menagerie to enter the city. This story (see *The History of the Westgate* by Goldney) was really somewhat absurd and improbable. The vehicles, or as it is sometimes stated, the elephants that were excluded from the city by the narrowness of the Westgate must have been of prodigious size, since the largest double-decker buses are able to come through at the present time. Again, this can have been no last-minute decision as it would have taken months to remove the largest and most substantial city gate in the country, which was then still in use as the city gaol. However, apart from the negative evidence of there being no reference to it in the minutes of the city council, one fact alone refutes this engaging legend; Wombwell died towards the end of 1850 and therefore the mayor referred to in the story must have been John Brent (elected 9th November 1849). Now John Brent was a keen antiquarian, and wrote a book *Canterbury in the Olden Time* published in 1860. There is no reference to the attempted removal of the Westgate in this book. Are we then to suppose that an ardent antiquary who had been responsible by his own vote for saving Canterbury's greatest civic monument from destruction would write a book about olden times and forget to mention such a remarkable occurrence?

Although a man of little importance, except in the local scene, Francis Bennett-Goldney's real character is as difficult to assess as that of Thomas Becket himself. How was such a devious and, it seems, unscrupulous person able to win and keep the confidence of so many people for so many years?

It is now over fifty years since he died, and there cannot be many people in Canterbury who knew him at first-hand; there are quite a few, however, who knew one of Goldney's greatest cronies, J. G. B. Stone, who survived until the 1950s and was fond of reminiscing about him. 'Stonie' as he was called, left a short memoire of his former associate which paints a far from flattering picture. Stone admired Goldney's handsome presence and engaging manners, and his sheer breathtaking audacity, but he acknowledges his foibles, particularly his weakness for humbug and intrigue. 'Stonie' implies that he himself had a hand in furthering Goldney's political plans, for which he was expelled from the local Conservative Club, and explains that his support did not stem entirely from 'unalloyed esteem and affection'; rather was Goldney seen as 'the only broom we could use to clean up the Augean stables of the old party, the filth of which had been accumulating since 1880, when the city was disfranchised for corruption and bribery and had no representative in the House of Commons for five years and fifty-seven days'.

Of one of Francis's weaknesses, in which he was the opposite of his predecessor Twyne, a little-known fact will give an obvious explanation. Twyne exposed the falsity of the fable that Canterbury was founded by 'Brutus' several centuries B.C., a fable invented by the notorious manufacturer of history, Geoffrey of Monmouth. Goldney invented the new myth about the saving of the Westgate in 1850. Although it has not been mentioned earlier, the fact is that Francis's father, Sebastian Evans, was also very much concerned in this fabrication. Now there is a very good translation of Geoffrey of Monmouth's works into English, the best in fact ever done. And the author? Sebastian Evans!

The very same man.

Perhaps Geoffrey's devotion to the gentle art of hoodwinking the public gradually seeped into the head of his translator Sebastian, who in turn passed it on to his ingenious son. It may be something of a comedown from King Arthur and the Holy Grail to the mayor of Canterbury and Wombwell's elephants, but with the material at their disposal Geoffrey's pupils did their best.

EIGHT

'ALMOST INTACT'

IN the early stages of Hitler's War, Canterbury was thought of and indeed officially classified as a safe area to which children could be sent from London under the evacuation scheme; this period of delusions and false hopes was aptly called 'the phoney war'. Once the real war began, in the spring of 1940, the south-east, and with it Canterbury, were seen to be not a haven but a death-trap, and it was not long before all but essential people were being sent away from the city.

The Battle of Britain began; the air-raid sirens wailed without ceasing, and many a hard-pressed German bomber, lightening ship to get away from the Spitfires, would jettison its deadly load on the city. But it was only when the reprisals known as the Baedeker raids were directed against historic towns that Canterbury experienced the full might of the Luftwaffe. Older citizens who saw the results are surprised and perhaps pained to find that their juniors are quite ignorant of these events, and are irritated when this ignorance is shared by architectural critics attacking the form of Canterbury's post-war development. One such article, published by a Canterbury organisation and typical of its *genre*, suggested that the city survived the war 'fairly intact', and went on to allege that no real attempt had been made to deal with the problems of a cathedral city. To speak thus is to disregard the factors that have decisively influenced the development of one-third of the centre of modern Canterbury, and to ignore the painful, but interesting, civic convulsions that preceded the work of reconstruction.

The arguments and disputes that took place between 1944 and 1949 may at first sight look trivial against the backcloth of Canterbury's immense panorama of time, but the critic must remember that these events, in the end, created much of the Canterbury that we see today and our descendants will see for some generations to come; and to the more thoughtful they provide a good case-history of the functioning of democratic government in a small community.

Those who think that the city survived the war fairly intact would be surprised to know that it received 445 high-explosive bombs, plus an estimated 10,000 incendiaries, and according to official figures 800 houses and other buildings were demolished, and another 1,000 seriously, and over 5,000 slightly, damaged. The city experienced 2,477 alerts and felt itself fortunate to escape with a mere 115 fatal casualties, plus some hundreds of injured.

Plans and photographs show the main shopping area on either side of St. George's Street almost completely destroyed, including St. George's church itself, of which only the tower remains, and that in a rickety condition. The area of devastation, whole or partial, extends to Watling Street on the south-west and to Burgate on the north-east. There is a further large swathe in St. George's Place, and again in Broad Street, with a smaller pocket of destruction in St. Dunstan's. Outside these more important sections of havoc the records can only mean that practically every house must have received damage in one form or another, and that there were few quarters of the town that escaped some measure of serious destruction. As well as St. George's church, that of St. Mary Bredin was completely destroyed; The Royal Fountain Hotel, the old coaching hostelry, was burnt to the ground, the Corn Exchange and Longmarket were gutted, the County Hall destroyed, and the birthplace of Marlowe went up in flames. Lady Wootton's Green, in front of the gateway to St. Augustine's, was destroyed except for one house, and the Fyndon Gateway itself seriously damaged and the roof of the ancient refectory displaced. In the Precincts, the Victorian cathedral library received a direct hit from a high explosive bomb, while canons' residences and buildings of the King's School were destroyed or seriously damaged. The roof of the Norman staircase received a thorough shake-up and the Kent War Memorial was peppered with flying fragments. As the cathedral itself received only superficial damage (though its preservation was partly due to the gallantry of the fireguards, who threw down incendiary bombs from the roofs oblivious of their own safety) the question has been asked whether the Germans were or were not trying to hit it. If they were, how

The city after the 1942 blitz
Modern shops now replace the ruins

could they have missed such an easy target? If they were not, then how came the bombs to fall within yards; on the library, canons' houses and the like? One is almost tempted to enquire whether St. Thomas may have been watching over the place of his martyrdom.

Critics frequently write as if no real thought had been given to the problems of reconstruction, and seem to be unaware that the rebuilding of Canterbury after the war caused one of the biggest and bitterest rows (and there have been plenty to chose from) in the whole history of the city.

At first, however, the omens were reasonably favourable. The city council tried by every device known to them, including public conferences, to consult anybody and everybody about the future, and hoped thereby to have the goodwill of most if not of all.

Unhappily, the chief official, George Woodfin Marks, town clerk, had been killed in the Baedeker raid in June 1942, but the war-time mayor, Charles Lefevre, a successful and public-spirited business man who had led the city for four years, was still there to pull the side together, and where necessary to reconcile warring factions.

A consultant planner was appointed. Dr. Charles Holden, nominated at the suggestion of the government by the Royal Institute of British Architects. Of ripe experience, he had designed the principal buildings of London University and of London Transport. Scholarly, competent and eminently reasonable, Holden seemed to be the right man in the right place.

At this epoch everyone was talking about a document called the Uthwatt Report, which put forward the novel idea that local authorities should be enabled to buy up the land in war-damaged areas at pre-war values and 'secure its proper redevelopment'. Legislation was impending. The city council pricked up their ears and started to follow the scent. They little suspected that it would end in a hornets' nest.

A character hanging about in the wings, but of whom Canterbury and Britain were soon to hear a good deal was a Mr. L. H. Wilson, an architectural assistant in the Canterbury city surveyor's department. At the same time as Dr. Charles Holden was appointed consultant, Mr. Wilson was given his own department as city architect.

Dr. Holden brought forward his proposals for redeveloping

o

Roman pavement found in Butchery Lane

the central area, which by now was an immense waste of weed-sprouting ruins, in advance of his plans for the rest of the city, in the month of February 1945. Sad to relate, whatever might be the international position there was no peace on the Canterbury planning front for at least five years after the publication of the Holden plan. The features that were destined to arouse desperate opposition included a new road parallel to the High Street, a monumental Civic Way, linking Cathedral and Civic Centre, and most unpopular of all, the idea of the purchase of the land in the damaged areas.

Trouble was not long in blowing up, for the Holden proposals alarmed powerful—and moneyed—interests both within and outside the city council. The latter had decided to hold a public conference to explain their plans and to invite comments and suggestions, but before this could take place there had been a public indignation meeting at which a Citizens' Defence Association had been formed to fight the council's plan to the death. The Corporation's conference was a complete failure so far as selling the plan to the public was concerned, and mayor Charles Lefevre said he was ashamed of the way that private interests had been put first and the welfare of the city a bad second.

The newly-formed Citizens' Defence Association told the city council that Holden's plan would destroy the traditional character of Canterbury, and that the acquisition of land in the damaged areas was a gross injustice to the owners. The editor of the principal local newspaper promised the Association his support in a full-blooded press campaign.

The first post-war election (in which, owing to the suspension of such elections during hostilities, half the city council were to face the voters) was due on the 1st of November; the new Association put up candidates in opposition to the plan, and the election was fought entirely on this issue and no other; the first time in the history of this country that such an event had taken place.

Then, after all these distant rumblings, the lightning struck. On the 17th October 1945, the mayor, Charles Lefevre, died, having succumbed to the strain of leading the city through upwards of four long years of stress and bombardment, a struggle to which he gave heart and soul. So the effective leader was gone.

The result was a disaster for those who favoured Holden's plan.

Every candidate who supported it was defeated, and every one
who opposed it, elected.

The new council quickly decided against buying up the bomb-
damaged area, a step that every other blitzed town was taking
under government recommendation, and referred the planning
proposals of Dr. Holden to a committee, which would go
through them line by line. This resulted in the deletion of the
parallel road and the wide Civic Way; but it is one thing to
condemn a plan in the emotional atmosphere of the hustings, and
quite another to assess it in the calm atmosphere of a committee room, and the new masters of the council found that there
was a good deal in the proposals that they could pass over in
consenting silence, and some that could actually be commended.
'The dominating character of the cathedral, the charm and
intimacy of the narrow streets and the ancient city walls must be
retained regardless of the restrictions to planning so imposed'—
unanimous approval for that. And the style of architecture for the
reconstruction was tacitly approved—'No mock mediaeval, no
flashy mannerisms or picturesque dummies, but the neighbourli-
ness and dignity of sane and orderly building'. And the committee nodded approvingly over the inner and outer ring roads
and sub-arterial radials linking them. They also passed over,
without dissent, Holden's denunciation of 'Vulgar shop-fronts'
installed by 'catch-penny shopfitters'.

The examination of Holden's plan took up weeks and months,
and in the meantime there were urgent problems to solve in the
city, including the major one of reviving its trade. Even temporary shops had to have sites, and it would have been against the
election pledges to buy them.

The council's difficulty was that they had secured election in
effect on one point, on which their hands were tied; but on other
things where no pledges had been given they acted as any normal
council would do. The saving grace of the new councillors was
that once away from their *idée fixe* about not 'expropriating' the
owners of the blitzed area their approach was, if anything, bolder
and more progressive than that of many of the councillors whom
they had replaced. When a Roman tessellated pavement was discovered by the archaeologists in Butchery Lane, and it was feared
that the pavement might be taken up and removed elsewhere,
they unhesitatingly stepped in with a compulsory purchase order
for the site, even though it was part of the disputed central area;

and as the pavement was eight feet or more below the modern street level, it was possible to build temporary shops above it, relieving the council of another embarrassing problem. Gradually the new men were learning the facts of life—the hard way. They were negotiating, for example, to take over an old and roomy house and convert it into flats when they discovered that Canon Shirley, Headmaster of the King's School, was about to whisk the prize from under their noses, so that he could add another boarding-house to the School's resources. Without hesitation, the councillors threatened to use their statutory powers of acquisition and thus forestalled the energetic canon. Farmers, loath to dispose of their orchards for the building of housing estates, and development companies holding on to tracts of desirable building land in the hopes of better terms in the future, were compelled to sell. And the same story was repeated, over and over again. In so far as Canterbury's new masters had held themselves up as being horrified at the idea of compulsory purchase, they strongly resembled the medieval friars with their vows of poverty. They discovered that for ordinary bread-and-butter local government services, such as a civic centre, car-parks and road widening, at least twelve acres of land in the sacred central area would be needed.

In truth, the only way in which the municipalisation of the damaged areas could be avoided was for all the owners to get together and pool their ownership under some private scheme, whose features would be at least as good as any scheme that the local authority could produce. In practice, this was virtually impossible, for the simple reason that the local authority had compulsory powers and the owners did not, so that if one single owner was not prepared to go along with the private scheme, it was torpedoed.

The pressure on the poor council became intolerable. As peacetime activities were resumed, the commercial interests wanted to rebuild and trade in the St. George's Street area, which before its destruction had been the finest shopping area in the city.

To make matters worse, the Ministry of Town and Country Planning would not look at the 'amendments' that the new council wished to make in Dr. Holden's plan, and on this matter the government had the final voice. In point of fact the 'new boys' were on the verge of cracking, and accepting the Holden plan, when the Ministry cracked first, owing to one of the country's periodical financial crises. All the blitzed towns were told to be less bold in their planning, and reminded of the virtues of economy and realism. Canterbury needed no such reminder, but in the usual somewhat ham-handed government way they were included as recipients of this advice, and in consequence were encouraged to put forward a new compromise with the principles of Holden; this the Ministry turned down flat.

By this time Hugh Wilson had been made jointly responsible with the city engineer for planning; he and the leading civil servants went quietly aside and hammered out the compromise. The parallel road remained, the Civic Way was out, St. George's Tower, a great stumbling-block, was in, the inner ring-road took a course immeasurably less destructive than Holden's line; in the detail there was more medieval sense of enclosure. This was Canterbury's last chance to avoid damaging and disastrous delay in rebuilding, and everyone knew it, and 'with our minds but not in our hearts' the councillors gave way to the inevitable. Minds or hearts, the votes were for Wilson's plan.

The Wilson plan was a road plan, and in agreeing it the city fathers had acquired a very nice skeleton. It now remained to clothe it with flesh, in the form of layouts of the building blocks, service roads and other features in the damaged area. This was now to be done 'in accordance with the best principles of planning without regard to the ownership of sites', but they still contemplated that somehow the former owners would retain their freeholds. However, the committee whose job it was to investigate ways and means reported that this was quite impracticable, and that after all the city council must acquire at least thirty acres of land in the war-damaged area.

The crunch had now come; the members who had been elected to oppose the Holden plan and the wholesale 'expropriation' of property owners in the war-damaged areas now knew that in principle both were inevitable. Their leader, Mr. Jennings, (destined to be Mayor of Canterbury in the course of a few years), went to the town clerk, placed all his cards on the table, and asked for advice. That official suggested the idea of a public meeting to sound out opinion. If the council could be satisfied that views had changed with the changing circumstances, then they would be acting quite honourably in departing to the extent of the change from their election pledges, their 'mandate'. This advice Mr. Jennings gratefully accepted.

The date of the meeting was 23rd March 1949, nearly seven years after the greatest of the air attacks, and almost four years after victory in Europe; and where better could such a meeting have been held than in the very lecture hall at the Beaney, where Canterbury had once made Charles Lefevre ashamed.

There was a full house, and everyone interested in the controversy seemed to be there (in Canterbury we all know one another). The councillors' dilemma had been explained at length; citizens had asked questions and had been answered, more or less satisfactorily; the time had come to find out what the assembled public would have to say about the proposal of their elected representatives: that they should wait for three months to see if anyone could by any manner of wit suggest a way of rebuilding Canterbury's bombed areas to modern standards without resort to the hated 'expropriation'; if at the end of that time no champion had come forward to show how this could be done, then the city fathers would, reluctantly, under the compulsion of events, and with heavy hearts, proceed to cut the Gordian knot with the sword of compulsory acquisition.

It was now up to the audience, and the platform waited anxiously to see which way it would go. Now that it had come to the test, the way out of the dilemma did not seem quite so clever. What if the plan backfired, and the citizens gave the wrong answer?

A gentleman jumped up and caught the mayor's eye. His business was that of a licensed victualler, and his shop was one of the properties threatened by the council's plans. This looked ominous, but the mayor had no option but to ask him to speak. He made no preliminary explanation, no reasoned exposé of his views, but said in a rather deferential manner that he would like, if it was in order, to move a resolution. Again the mayor could only nod the invitation to proceed.

'I move,' said the citizen, '*that you forget about the three months, and get on with the job within one month.*'

What sounded like an ominous even threatening murmur, arose from the assembled townspeople; but it was impatience, not anger, that they were expressing. When the motion was put, a forest of hands went up in favour; not a single soul voted against. The few C.D.A. stalwarts could only sit glum; after less than four years their once powerful movement was shown up as a paper tiger.

The mandate was dead.

The 'designation' of the thirty acres then proceeded peacefully, and Whitehall sanctioned the purchase of a third of this area in advance on grounds of urgency.

An attractive feature of Canterbury's rebuilt central area is the tower of the bombed church of St. George, which has been retained. Its preservation, however, was something of an accident. It was thought, quite wrongly as we now know, that to keep the tower would mean sterilising quite a large and valuable shopping frontage, and the city council was opposed to this (so incidentally was the Citizens' Defence Association) but owing to the technicalities of the planning legislation, government planners were able to insist on the tower's being retained, on the ground that its doorway showed it to be a relic of the Norman period. Canterbury then insisted on the Ministry's paying for the restoration work (further technicalities involved in this). After the government had spent £13,000, it was found that the Norman doorway was not a part of the tower at all and not even bonded into it. The government people were exceeding wroth, went into a fit of sulks, and stopped work for some time, but eventually agreed to continue as it was impossible to leave the job half finished. However, the tower having been kept, Wilson advised that it must be made an attractive feature, and Mr. Peter Shepheard, future president of the R.I.B.A. and a renowned landscaper, was retained to prepare a treatment. The paved sunken garden, the tinted pavement and the two whitebeam trees that give such a charming effect today are the results of Shepheard's work.

To complete the planning job, a development plan for the whole city had to be adopted. This gave the chance for the revival of all the old arguments, but only a handful of irreconcilables continued the hopeless fight, and in due course the plan gained approval.

Armed with powers of acquisition of the damaged area, with the layout plan approved, and with everyone apparently eager to go, the city fathers might well have hoped, or in one or two cases feared, that the end was now in sight. But more unexpected troubles descended upon them. First, a spectacular and prolonged row arose over the appearance and style of architecture of the new buildings. The Ministry, as is not unusual, behaved with some lack of consistency. In spite of repeated appeals for guidance they failed entirely, for at least a twelve-month, to state their policy on the vital question of the style and appearance of the rebuilt area. When they finally did come to a decision, it was with the threat that unless the city satisfied the Minister that they were acting properly, he would take over the planning decisions himself—a little hard on people who had been trying to find out what the Minister wanted for so long.

However, after a certain amount of acerbity, the difficulty was sorted out, and it was agreed that the city architect should prepare what was called a 'street picture'—a great expression in those times, before such ones as 'the Environment' had been popularised—for St. George's Street, and submit it to the Royal Fine Art Commission. If they approved of it, all the plans for buildings in the street would have to fit into it; and then no doubt, if anyone complained to the Minister about them, the Minister would be able to blame the Commission.

Hugh Wilson proposed, and the Royal Fine Art Commission accepted, that the new buildings should be designed 'in a lively contemporary manner', and recommended the 'massing'—another vogue word of those years—which was in fact followed in the design of the street as we see it today; the larger and more important units ranged on one side, forming a dramatic composition with St. George's tower and its surrounding garden; the other side quieter, with smaller standard shops linked and unified by a colonnade.

It was the colonnade that caused the last big flare-up in Canterbury's prolonged saga of planning conflict. For some reason it raised the angriest passions and things reached such an impasse that it seemed that the £140,000 worth of building work authorised—at that time a licence was needed to spend more than £100 on such work—would have to be postponed indefinitely, and the allocation of licences to that amount lost. The city architect was begged to modify his views about the colonnaded shops, and in spite of his having told the members on his appointment that he would accept no direction on aesthetic matters, he agreed to bend. He good-humouredly suggested a few superficial alterations, and thereby got the plans approved after all, but the colonnade to which he attached great importance remained. Some of his superficial modifications were quietly left out when the shops went up, and no one noticed the omission.

The elevational crisis was thus settled; everybody breathed

afresh; the licences could be taken up after all, building could go on, and Canterbury could be revived.

Finally, in 1952 a new society called the Canterbury Preservation Society, now the Canterbury Society, was founded to replace the Citizens' Association, as the C.D.A. was eventually renamed. A year later, the Labour Government having gone out of office, and Mr. Silkin having retired to the House of Lords, his Lordship came to Canterbury with Lady Silkin to see how the city was getting on, and was much impressed with what he saw.

And Mr. Wilson? His Canterbury trials and tribulations did him no harm; the Ministry were impressed, especially the Permanent Secretary, Dame Evelyn (now Baroness) Sharp, and they persuaded him to enter the New Towns sphere. After designing Cumbernauld, and assisting with a few more, he took the plunge into private work, amassed a vast practice, and eventually came to the presidency of the R.I.B.A. Many years after he left the city the Queen made him a knight. But it was at Canterbury that he won his spurs.

STONIE

An unforeseen result of the acrimonious dispute that broke out over the rebuilding of Canterbury after its war damage was the return to prominence of a character whose active days should, according to the normal course of nature, have long been ended—Councillor John George Bosworth Stone.

In 1945 Mr. Stone was over eighty years of age, and had been a member of the city council since 1899 continuously. Short and stocky, with the head of an ancient Roman senator and the voice of a fog-horn, with a bright eye and a weather-beaten countenance, 'Stonie' was the only member of the council who had, in his prime, been well known in local government circles outside those of Canterbury and Kent. Self-made and self-taught, he was an assiduous student of law and local government, and loved to be photographed in his study, emphasising a point with the stem of his pipe against a background of shelves crammed with the volumes of Lumley's Public Health, Arnold's Law of Municipal Corporations and other learned tomes.

It is related that when a new councillor asked Stone to lend him a book that he might profitably read to inform himself of his duties and responsibilities, the sage suggested that he should hire a pantechnicon and bring it round to the house-and-shop in Palace Street where 'Stonie' lived.

His career in local government was exceptional, and possibly unique in its length. He was to survive to the year 1957, by which time he was aged ninety-four, and had spent nearly sixty years as a council member.

In his heyday he had been something of a national figure in his chosen sphere. A guardian, as well as a councillor, he was equally expert on poor law, rating and assessment, and the functions of the watch committee, of which he was, for many years, the chairman. In the old days poor law and rating were closely connected, and Stone had the great honour of serving as a member of the Central Valuation Committee, a body of hand-picked experts whose duty it was to give advice to rating authorities throughout the country, so as to secure some measure of uniformity in the days when each area did its own rating.

In police matters, Stone was a martinet, and would tolerate no inefficiency. At least one chief constable was eased out of office by his implacable manœuvring.

Stone was a tailor in a small way, and his means remained modest to the end. His iron integrity would not permit him to make a halfpenny out of his public activities. In seventeen successive elections he was returned unopposed, and as time went on, because of his exhaustive knowledge of Canterbury and its families and their little secrets, he became the most feared man in the city, though the only direct use he ever made of his knowledge would be some cutting, *sotto voce* aside.

He first made his name as a public figure when he joined the guardians, at a time when Canterbury was plagued with a large number of tramps. The new guardian went to the casual ward of the workhouse to inspect the night's intake of wayfarers.

'Why are you on the road?' he asked each in turn.

'Looking for work' was the usual reply.

'You've found it,' said Stone, pointing to an enormous pile of wood that he had caused to be assembled, which the visitors were required to chop up next morning before being allowed to proceed on their way. The number of tramps coming to Canterbury then decreased dramatically, according to Stone's account.

But this was many years ago. Stone was always ready to give credit where credit was due, and liked to tell the story of the very upright chief constable, who when a case of whisky was sent to him for Christmas, together with a cake for his men, ordered the cake to be sent back because the police did not accept gifts.

His association with the devious and flamboyant Bennett-Goldney has already appeared; one of Stone's mementos was a photograph of himself with Bennett-Goldney on the Duke of Bedford's yacht *Sapphire* navigating the Solent in 1912.

Another strange episode in the life of the Father of the Canterbury City Council was when he stumped the country as an economist, before World War I, to campaign for tariff reform. He sometimes spoke of the development to his powers of oratory occasioned by haranguing groups of steelworkers in the teeth of a gale outside the factory gates of Sheffield and Rotherham.

'Stonie' despised humbug; when one alderman was being congratulated on the receipt of a not very high honour, Stone in an ostensibly fulsome speech quoted Mark Twain's remark about the Legion of Honour: 'few escape that distinction'. On another similar occasion he could be heard, but only by his immediate neighbours, muttering something about 'saponacious panegyrics'.

He refused to be placed in a position which made him dependent on his fellow councillors. For this reason he would not accept an aldermanic robe, still less the office of mayor. He was, however, prevailed on to receive the honorary freedom of the city, on the distinct understanding that there should be no expense on a casket for the scroll, or on attendant junketing.

This then was the man who, in 1945, threw aside the role of elder statesman and cross-bencher, and waded in to take part in the fierce controversies that had developed over the planning and rebuilding of the city.

Whatever advanced age had taken from Councillor Stone, it had not deprived him of his sense of timing. At the last meeting of the wartime city council in 1945, it was he who moved the amendment to postpone the proposal to apply for powers to purchase the blitzed area. With cynical effrontery the old rascal admitted that he had nothing against the planning scheme, nor for it for that matter, yet affected the part of a father confessor.

'You have called me Father of the Council,' he declared. 'If ever I have had a fatherly feeling for you, I have it today . . . If you approve my amendment, no elector will be able to point a finger at those seeking re-election to the Council and say that they forced the scheme down the ratepayers' throats before they had a chance of protesting.'

To Stone's well-simulated emotion (anyone knowing the man knew that beyond the pleasure of having his own way, it was a matter of indifference to him which way the thing went) even the more phlegmatic members succumbed, and no one at all risked the finger of scorn by voting against his amendment. This manœuvre contributed to the postponement of the rebuilding of Canterbury for some years.

Stone was nothing if not destructive. When in 1945 the new and inexperienced 'anti-plan' councillors were sent to the municipal buildings by the electors, he was in his element. To these neophytes he appeared omniscient on all local government themes, and he took full advantage of their credulity.

There was no vice in the man, but in his dotage he just could not refrain from mischief; one example was when the conscientious, kindly and well-meaning Mr. Silkin, the Minister of Town and Country Planning in the Labour Government, wanted to find out what was going on in the towns that had serious war-damage problems, including Canterbury. Egged on by Stone, the city council snubbed the Minister and refused to meet him. This unworthy action may have given the members the feeling that they were fine fellows, but even Stone's new dupes could not swallow the studiedly insulting words that he wished to add to the resolution; not to be put off, he simply gave them to the press.

Whenever really important decisions were to be made, however, Stone was usually absent or silent, perhaps biding his time, perhaps indifferent.

The last great furore in which he took part was the row over the proposed colonnaded shops in St. George's Street, when he intervened with some bombastically-worded rescinding motion to cancel the approval already given to the shops; a thing which it is quite impossible for a local authority to do without ministerial consent and payment of astronomical compensation. Stone really knew little, and cared less about planning.

Almost to the end he stayed active and healthy. When approaching ninety, he was knocked off his bicycle in St. Margaret's Street, and hit his head on the kerb. Surely, people thought, this must be the end. But the most marked result of his serious injuries was that everyone who visited him in the Kent and Canterbury hospital had to inspect the bloodstained jacket in which he had sustained his accident, which (shades of Erasmus) was kept in a cupboard at the bedside for this purpose.

The nurses found him a handful. Against their instructions, he insisted on going along the passage for necessary purposes; when his bed was found empty by the night sister, she tapped on the door behind which the patient had presumably concealed himself, and said softly, 'Mr. Stone, you will be getting me into trouble.' Came the reply from within: 'What! At my age?'

Eventually in his ninety-fifth year, Stone's hour came, and he knew it.

'I am going to meet my Maker,' he confided to his sympathising friends, 'and I can't say I am looking forward to the interview.'

One wonders how the Almighty and he got on together.

NINE

ONWARD FROM THEODORE

CANTERBURIANS of the 1930s or at least those of them who had any civic pride, must have looked back wistfully to the good old days when the city, as well as being famous for its national shrine, was also one of the half-dozen or so most prominent towns of the realm in its own right.

The cradle of the nation's spiritual enlightenment, to use Dr. Temple's phrase, had been of old a rich and important city besides; as late as the sixteenth century, with pilgrimages a thing of the past, had not Queen Bess held her court here, and even in the not-so-good days of the seventeenth, when the divine right of kings was called so violently into question, had not Cavaliers and Roundheads schemed, plotted, intrigued, rioted and fought for control of the ancient city, esteeming it a noteworthy and valuable prize?

But two-and-a-half centuries of decline, which Walloons, hop-growers, soldiery, and later cricketers could only partially redeem, had left the place ecclesiastically important, but apart from its function as a market town, economically insignificant. To the thoughtful this seemed wrong; the city of Ethelbert, of Becket and of Marlowe deserved more than memories to support its dignity. The time had surely come to end the retreat, turn about and advance to a more prosperous future. But what should be the rallying-cry, and who should give it?

An unexpected volunteer came forward—in the person of Corporal Adolf Hitler. The experience of having a large slice of the city knocked flat by the Luftwaffe seemed to act as a tonic, and the people of Canterbury were not content just to put back what had been destroyed (although that itself caused quite enough trouble as we have heard), but determined to build a better and finer city, and to look for expansion.

Listening to the clichés of the present rather than to the voice of history, they first sought to attract light industry, ignoring the facts that factories at Whitstable or Herne Bay were as good for Canterbury as factories in Canterbury; that the government with its policy of helping depressed areas was dead against them; that Canterbury was in the wrong position with the great mass of London blocking it off from the markets of the Midlands and North; and that it had no industrially trained labour-force, only a limited number of women looking for pin money. Buildings sprouted on the small industrial estates, but the only industries were the noisy metal works and saw mills, decanted from other parts of the city to a place where they would be less of a nuisance to their neighbours; the rest were mere distribution centres for products from paint to spare parts, from mineral water to steel rods, no doubt strengthening the city's role as a market town, but nothing more.

History, had she been consulted, could have suggested the answer to the search for a suitable direction for the city's advance, because in the 1840s and 1850s three things had happened which showed that the dispensing of enlightenment from Canterbury need not be thought to have ended with the conversion of the English to Christianity: on the ruins of St. Augustine's Abbey a missionary college was built; on St. Thomas's Hill to the north the Clergy Orphan Corporation established St. Edmund's School; and in the Precincts of the Cathedral the King's School was transformed from a mainly local to a nationally known public school.

The new college at St. Augustine's, inspired by the Kent Member of Parliament, Beresford Hope, was the work of a well-known Victorian architect, William Butterfield, and we are told that he followed this effort with what is regarded as his masterpiece, All Saints, Margaret Street, London. Keble College, Oxford, was another of his works but is not, it would seem, considered to be a masterpiece.

At Canterbury, William Butterfield used to a large extent the medieval foundations for his buildings; the library, for instance, was on the site of the abbot's guest hall; other guest accommodation was used or adapted to supply a refectory and a chapel. The story of the college is a sad one. Tablets in the chapel recall the careers of the missionaries, and many of them did not last long in the white man's graveyard. Eventually the demand slackened so much that the first purpose of Butterfield's college was changed, and the church used it for the training of ordinary stay-at-home clergy. It had a brief career as the central post-ordination college of the Anglican Communion, but the funds dried up, and the buildings are now used by King's College, London, though still for ordination courses.

Architects wax expressive but obscure when they come to describe the style of the building of knapped flint with stone dressings. They are 'Butterfield's most likable work', fair enough; 'primitive of the high Victorian'; 'the ecclesiologists favourite architect'; 'the return to the earlier and more robust middle pointed style'. Architects will perhaps understand these expressions; others, with acknowledgments to Edward Gibbon, can only try to remember them.

About the time when Butterfield was busy at St. Augustine's, the Clergy Orphan Corporation were building their new school on the heights of St. Thomas's Hill overlooking Canterbury from the north, and their enterprise gave Canterbury its second public school, St. Edmund's. The architect, well known in his profession, had just designed, it seems, the Great Western Hotel in London, and the critic frowningly remarks that by comparison St. Edmund's is eclectic and hardly typical of the time; and the buildings were constructed of Kentish rag with Bath stone dressings. It is noteworthy in having the lower half in English Gothic style and the upper in French.

After sundry vicissitudes, including wartime evacuation with the King's School to Cornwall, the school, in contrast to the missionary college, continues to flourish.

The King's School must be an even hardier plant if it is true as many people assert that it is the oldest school in England, founded in A.D. 600. The pros and cons of this controversy have been ventilated pretty thoroughly in our study of the exploits of John Twyne, and need not detain us here. In any case the King's School has little need to press the perhaps debatable claim when it has an authentic history of over 432 years, since 1541, packed with incident, enough to satisfy any well-conducted academy. In this time the school has progressed from the fifty scholars endowed by Henry VIII to the present 680, from John Twyne's single school house to John Shirley's empire of half the Precincts with subsidiary dominions in the suburbs of Canterbury, the village of Sturry and the fields of Hackington; from attachment to the apron-strings of the Dean and Chapter to in-

Modern chapel of Christ Church College
Science Building at the university

dependence and secure tenancy of houses, property and playing fields, under Royal Charter handed over by King George VI in person.

Dr. Mitchinson was Canterbury's Dr. Arnold. An energetic realist, he saw clearly that in the railway age a school, if it was not to sink into a purely local role, must have a national reputation, and that being a local school meant living on the skim with the nationally-known places taking the cream. Generations later John Shirley put a shrewd business head at the school's service. He did not escape criticism; no man of action, of boundless energy and determination, can expect to do that, but he delivered the goods, and under his drive the school reached new heights of academic and sporting success, vast increases in numbers and revenue, and as a final goal, that precious Charter of independence from the old gentlemen in the Chapter Office.

Whatever may be the statistics of numbers of scholarships, of cricket matches won, a school must be judged by the end product, the men it produces. The two Elizabethans, Marlowe and Harvey, would be a sufficient ration of greatness for any school, and some of the moderns Walter ('hard gem-like flame') Pater, Hugh Walpole, and Somerset Maugham are well-known writers of only the second rank. We are not thinking, however, of the occasional man of genius whom the school is lucky enough to have, but of the run-of-the-mill pupils. At the King's School, at least one archbishop, one Lord Chief Justice and one Lord Chancellor lead a host of clergy, missionaries, colonial administrators and Oxford dons who make up a large part of the yearly outflow. Even the cocky knocker for six of Rommel, the inimitable 'Monty', had one term at the junior school.

Not content with this galaxy some enthusiasts are working hard on the theory that the brother of Sir Francis Drake was at the school. They would be better advised to leave the topic of circumnavigation to the Simon Langton school, which can claim in the person of Sir Alec Rose, not the brother of the man who has achieved this, but the man himself.

And the King's School has yet another trick up its sleeve. It can reinforce the long roll of the factually famous with a short but distinguished fictitious list; David Copperfield, no less, and Philip Carey. Copperfield, you may remember, went to a school in the precincts of the cathedral kept by Dr. Strong. There is only one school in the precincts now, and apart from the choir school,

10

University Senate House
Rutherford College at the university

there never has been more than one. Our friend Philip came a
good deal later, bearing a name which, though less familiar to the
reading public, in fact thinly disguises the autobiographical ego of
Somerset Maugham. Poor Philip did not enjoy himself very
much at the school, but then he never seems to have settled down
either at 'Tercanbury' or at 'Blackstable', where he stayed with
his uncle. For Philip, or shall we call him Willie, recollections of
the school must have mellowed with advancing age, and his
ashes are buried near the Norman staircase.

After the Missionary College was built at St. Augustine's there
remained within the ancient Precinct of the Abbey a large tract
of land unused except for market gardening, and in one corner a
building which ended up as a banana warehouse. Some time after
Hitler's war, the government of the day (in one of those periodic
rushes of blood to the head) panicked, and decided that enormous
numbers of extra school teachers were required, much more than
could be trained in the colleges as they were then. The Church of
England decided to tip in, and apart from sundry enlargements
here and there, screwed up its courage to build one completely
new college. By a piece of remarkable prescience the land in
St. Augustine's precinct had been labelled in the town planning
scheme as reserved for a major educational project, and lo and
behold, as rarely happens in matters of planning, such a project
was now mooted, and what better place could there be for the
new college than in St. Augustine's old Monastery and within
sight of Bell Harry.

But trouble arose from the life cycle of the common banana.
One would not believe it, but elaborate and expensive machinery
is needed to keep the banana in trim, and with sinking heart the
Church of England people found that they were faced with an
enormous bill to get rid of the warehouse, which was too big to
plan around; and even if some ingenious architect could have
made such a plan, wholesale trafficking in bananas is scarcely a
good mix with the training of teachers for Church of England
schools. However, the municipal authorities worked out what
it was really worth to Canterbury on a sheer money basis alone
to have such a college, and offered a pretty generous grant so
that the church was able to buy out the banana merchant. So the
land was bought and Christ Church College built. It is a splendid
piece of modern architecture, with a magnificent chapel of

unusual design, and has been so successful that extensions have been required. When offering their help the city council acted not only with enlightened self-interest, but also as if they had at last read the lessons of history. But even better was to come.

The days of Theodore, or even of Theobald, were too far away to keep alive in Canterbury the idea of what the medieval people called a *studium generale*, and what today we call a university. A mere forty years ago such an idea to most Canterbury people would have seemed quite impracticable, but in the general euphoria of high achievement which Canterbury enjoyed as it surmounted its post-war problems and difficulties a pipe-dream flitted before men's eyes which gradually coalesced into an ambition, and from ambition was unbelievably carried into fulfilment.

The vigour that supported the project of a university stemmed from the experience of building and rebuilding a dozen schools, and from the width of vision which the evolution of its Art College in particular opened before Canterbury's eyes. The arty-crafty college where amateurs pottered and potted in the building that Sydney Cooper, the Victorian artist, gave to the city, had a dose in the 1950s of the medicine that Dr. Mitchinson had given to the King's School a hundred years earlier; the college grew less and less local and more and more national, and won a European reputation for graphic design. So when the pipe-dreamers saw the blue smoke resolving itself into shapes—of a university in the south of England; of a university in Kent with perhaps the odd faculty, say for theology or arts, at Canterbury; and finally of a complete university which might, if the cards were played right, be in or very near to the city—Canterbury did not hesitate, but strode boldly in to try its luck.

The formation of a modern university is a ponderous, lengthy and intricate exercise, and involves making a microcosm of the social elements of the chosen area, instilling it with enthusiasm and strengthening its determination to achieve the goal. The sponsors of a university, which in the modern rite are the first embodiment of the movement to establish it, will include a large number of academics, each one of whom thinks himself a good deal cleverer than all the other ones, and also a variegated lay element, from the House of Lords represented by the county aristocracy, to the shop-floor nobility represented by the trade unions. If all goes well the sponsors will turn themselves into a provisional committee, and the provisional committee into an interim council or governing body. The sponsors have first to sell their project to the central government. In these enlightened days there is neither king, nor pope, nor cardinal to endow a college or a seat of learning, but only the taxpayer, whose hard-earned money is syphoned off in copious quantities by the tax-gatherer and channelled by civil servants in whatever direction their political masters think will win most votes. There must obviously be some kind of machinery to administer this excellent system, and the doling out of money for universities is in the hands, most appropriately, of the University Grants Committee—a fifty-fifty amalgam of bureaucrats and egg-heads. These then are the people to hear the sponsors' case and to test the weight of the proffered moneybags that the supporters have supplied; to say whether it proves enough local interest; to satisfy themselves that the location is right; to recommend whether it shall be thumbs up or thumbs down.

The sponsors who had organised themselves to press for a university in Kent had therefore to pick a site before they could go to the Grants Committee with their case, and having combed their own county from end to end, came almost as an after-thought to have a look at that other county that Edward IV had made, the County of the City of Canterbury. They may have looked askance at the creation of the monarch who put to death the pious founder of Eton and of King's College, Cambridge. But to Canterbury they came; and they saw—could they be conquered? They scarcely concealed their scepticism when they were told that for all the impediments (such as the sacrosanctity of high-class agricultural land and of military training areas, and the tendency of the River Stour to flood its banks) which placed vast tracks of the city out of consideration, there were still no less than six sites eminently suitable for their purpose from which to make a choice. City officials took the Kent sponsors on a tour of the city, looking in at one site after another in reverse order of merit. Long before they reached the sixth and best the visitors freely admitted that the less good propositions were better than anything else they had seen in the county of Kent. The most favoured locality was in the parish of Hackington (about half a mile from the spot on which Archbishop Baldwin had wished to set up the Hackington College which the monks of Christ Church so selfishly opposed, and which the Pope countermanded in the twelfth century). The last stage of the journey took the party past the ancient church of St. Stephen, which now gives it name to the district, through the village green over-looked by Sir Roger Manwood's fifteenth-century almshouses and the half-timbered glebe cottage, and up St. Stephen's Hill to the crest of the downs that skirt Canterbury to the north. As they walked in the meadow and looked around them they had an uncanny feeling of being in the auditorium of an open-air theatre in which a magnificent spectacle was being displayed. The flat table-land on the crest gave way to a gently sloping belt of meadow about a quarter of a mile wide, flanked to left and to right by groves of trees, and terminated two or three hundred yards down the hill by another belt of woodland. The meadow-land was an auditorium, the belts of trees the sides, and the wood-land in front the footlights, of a gigantic open-air stage on which was displayed, like a model, the city of Canterbury with the cathedral in its midst; the details of house and shop and college and church and ancient tower softened by waves and spires of greenery threading between the buildings. The view down the valley to the right ended at Chartham, three or four miles distant, but to the left the power station at Pegwell Bay thirteen miles away was clear to see, with a glimpse of the chalk cliffs of Ramsgate beyond, and in the immediate foreground was the Norman church of St. Stephen.

The view left the sponsors breathless, and when they had recovered it was to gasp thankfully: 'Our search is ended'.

Thus was born the University of Kent at Canterbury.

The cumbrous title of the new institution is the result of a difference between those of the sponsors who wished the place to be called 'Kent', and others, predominantly the very eminent academics from Oxbridge, who had been called in to advise, and who would have plumped for 'Canterbury'. One has a certain sympathy with the county officials who had done an immense amount of spade-work, and provided the academic expertise so necessary to get such an important project on its feet. They had cheerfully accepted the choice of Canterbury (which is not part of the administrative county) as the seat of the university, and perhaps they were only human in rebelling against the omission of Kent's name from its title. 'The University of Kent at Canterbury' was adopted as a compromise, not altogether to their satisfaction.

It is related that when a certain borough wished to send an invitation to the vice-chancellor of the university, its town clerk, careful as such officials invariably are, rang up the county education department (who he presumed would know) to find out the exact designation of the intended guest.

When told 'The Vice-Chancellor of the University of Kent at Canterbury', he said, 'I don't want to know the address, I just want to know his title.'

'That is his title,' explained the Kent official. 'Here, we call it Boyle's law.'

The university opened its doors in October 1965, and by October 1972 there were 2,200 undergraduates and 400 postgraduate students, with an academic staff of 400, in addition to some 750 manual, technical, clerical and other workers. The meadow still slopes down towards the city, but the skyline is now guarded by the twin bastions, compact in design and clad in off-white reconstructed stone, of Eliot and Rutherford colleges, with brown brick, Y-shaped Darwin on their left as you look towards the cathedral. Keynes, away to the west, more conventional with its quadrangle, is hidden by trees and by Eliot. A million square feet of floor space is shared by the colleges, the scientic and research buildings, the senate house, the library, the registry, the sports centre and the Gulbenkian Theatre.

No undertaking, however gigantic, can transform Canterbury so long as it has its cathedral and its ancient streets, and remains the See of the Primate of All England; and in the first few years the impact of the university was about as great as if a couple of old ladies had opened a new café in the High Street.

Fellowship between Town and Gown was not helped by the way in which the university developed physically. A brilliant Whitehall invention, the self-cancelling decision, meant that the beautiful level fields between Whitstable Road and St. Stephen's (hitherto sacrosanct as a green belt, but selected for university playing fields) would be used for house-building instead. Before the university was thought of, civil servant A decided that the fields ought to be kept, open and unbuilt-on, as agricultural land, and all pleas to be allowed to cash-in on the high price of building-land by developing them were sternly rejected. When the university was mooted, civil servant B decided that the building of a nationally-planned university was permissible where ordinary houses would be barred; and that this went for our beautiful level fields, which accordingly became part of the university site. Then civil servant C trumped both his colleagues' aces; he decided that if they were to be bought for the university, the fields must be paid for as land that would otherwise have been available for *housing*. This meant that the university could not have them, because civil servant D next said that there was no possible chance of the government providing money to pay for any part of the university site at housing-land rate! And, as the owners had decided to give up their agricultural activities, there was nothing left to do but to build houses after all.

So, in effect, the university was pushed bodily away from the city; and the internal planning of the project tended to further the centrifugal tendency. A spinal road was built, descending gently from the heights to link up with Whitstable Road, and designed to have colleges strung out along its flanks, but the colleges never came; the architects found it easier to spread northward over the flat table-land, all the time edging away from Canterbury. Again, the cold discipline of the academic specialist seemed to have little in common with the warm humanity of the city's traditional life; any idea of naming the colleges after the great historical figures of city or cathedral was ridiculed; and for the first, and probably the only, time in recorded history, the sacred wish of the students was disregarded when they plumped for 'Becket College' as the name of the college that is now called 'Darwin'.

But the collision of ideas and attitudes between Gown and Town was only delayed by these circumstances; the academic influence soon became noticeable and finally, in some spheres, decisive.

There were numbers of students in Canterbury before it ever had a university and even today, if all the part-timers are roped in, together with the whole-time would-be architects, teachers, and graphic designers, it is clear that the 2,500 university students do not add up to fifty per cent of the total; but, certain it is that added to the others they fill up every available bed-sitter and ensure that any landlady willing to take lodgers never goes short of clients. Planners have to decide how many students are needed to turn a private house into a guest house; this change a planning permission must sanctify.

The university passengers, both students and their teachers, have certainly rocked the local government boat of Canterbury.

Opinions will differ as to whether it is right that young people coming to a city to spend about half of three successive years there, to study largely at the taxpayers' expense, should be enrolled as city voters, but by a surprising decision the courts have held that they should. This irruption of young people who have no permanent roots in the city, together with the thirst for municipal honours of some of their instructors, has given Canterbury its biggest electoral convulsion since the days of the Citizens' Defence Association. The city council as it is now constituted, along with all other city councils in England and Wales outside London itself, is under sentence of death; but for the last two years of its life it has come under the rule for the first time of the Labour Party.

Perhaps it is fitting that as the City of Canterbury as a unit of self-government slips quietly below the horizon, our eyes should be solaced by the view of a glorious Red sunset and our ears instructed by the non-stop commentary of a team of left-wing university lecturers—with perhaps the Professor of Classics, if there is one, murmuring to himself a line of Catullus: *Soles occidere et redire possunt.**

The sun of Canterbury can indeed, and will, rise again.

---

* Suns may set and rise again.

TEN

LIVING WITH THE PAST

THAT Canterbury people do not take themselves or their history too seriously is shown by the story of the Little Muse.

The friends of Marlowe's memory, many years ago, decided to collect a sum of money to build a worthy memorial to their hero. They received permission to place in the ancient Buttermarket, on a pedestal, a bronze statue of a little Muse with an inscription dedicating it to Kit Marlowe's memory. Round the sides there were miniature bronze statuettes of various famous actors portraying roles from the plays. So Marlowe was fittingly remembered before the portal of Christchurch Gateway, which was built only a matter of years after his death.

Then came the Great War of 1914. After the suffering and sacrifice the citizens wished to use this hallowed spot for building a memorial to the dead of Canterbury. So, with a sigh, the city fathers decided that the little Muse must go.

But perhaps she did not mind, because they took her to a picturesque setting in the Dane John, where she looked over some of the greenest grass in England and some of the prettiest flowers. And so, again, Kit Marlowe was remembered, most appropriately.

Then came another war, the war of Hitler. This time it was direct violence that struck the little Muse, not peaceful eviction. A German plane planted a stick of high explosive bombs right across the Dane John, shaking the city wall to its foundations and blowing the poor little Muse clean off her pedestal. Reverent hands rescued her, and it was found that apart from a few strings missing from her lyre she was pretty well intact. They carried her gently to a cellar in the basement of the city council's offices, where she remained safe and sound amid the later alarums and excursions of World War II. Then peace at last, and the little Muse was brought from her resting place. The masons deputed to put her back on her pedestal inquired which way the statue should face. An official whom they consulted was fairly sure that he knew which way she was facing before the air raid, but thought it might be better if she faced the other way. Instead of looking over the greensward and all those beautiful flowers, why not have her looking towards the pathway on which the public were wont to perambulate, whence she would make a delightful picture with such a colourful backcloth? So again Marlowe, our beloved Kit, was fittingly commemorated.

And so it would have stayed, but for the overzealous attentions of his admirers. One day the Marlowe Society, possibly descendants of the people who had put the statue in the Buttermarket so many years ago, came to celebrate the birthday of the poet. They brought a magnificent wreath of flowers. A few appropriate words were said, and then the president came forward to place the wreath—in front? Or behind? Which is the front? Which is the back? Here is the inscription to Kit Marlowe; place the wreath beneath it. But no; that is most inappropriate—to put it where one is looking at the charming little buttocks of the Muse. Go back to the front and lay it as an offering which she will smilingly oversee. But there is no inscription there. It looks as if you are placing the wreath as a tribute to the Muse, and not to Marlowe; his name is wreathless. Take it round to the back again . . . It still does not look right.

History does not report exactly what they did in the end. Perhaps they put the wreath at the side, or perhaps they went and bought a second wreath, and put one at the back and one at the front, one for the Muse, and one for poor neglected Kit.

But justice for Marlowe was at hand. A reporter from a national newspaper made a very good story of the wreath-laying ceremonial, and a week later the masons came back, unshipped the poor little Muse and turned her round, so that now you can put a wreath below Marlowe's inscription and do honour to the little Muse as well.

Mind you, almost any member of the Canterbury establishment would be offended if you suggested that he was not as conscious as he should be of the honour of living in an ancient city with great traditions.

'But, my dear sir,' he would probably retort, 'every time I have an important speech to make, on a big occasion, I always try to get hold of something apposite to quote from our ancient records. What do you think we keep a city archivist for?'

He might have added that the upper crust turn out loyally to applaud at mayor-making, to eat the mayor's *sole meunière*, *poulet rôti*, and *coupe jaques*, and drink Pouilly-Fuissé at his banquet, and to laugh and clap when an apoplectic town sergeant, his worship being about to speak, manages to extort a couple of brazen notes from the Burghmote horn. And when Cricket Week comes round, the same people will willingly consume cocktails, ice cream, and if they are lucky, Scotch salmon mayonnaise at the mayor's tent.

The views and practice of the business community are somewhat ambivalent. As a general rule they would claim to leave the traditions of the city in the safe hands of the city fathers. 'After all, it's their job; or rather it was until this present lot got in.' The gibe is, alas, not unmerited. Some of the new generation of city councillors have been observed to prefer the purple chiffon cravat to the regulation white tie, and yellow velveteen jacket and trousers to the sober blue robe of the councillor, even if, to compensate, the male hair style is distinctly medieval.

At the same time, the business life of the city is shot with reflections of a bygone age, the traders having long concluded that, in small doses, tradition is good for business. The names of Chaucer and Marlowe seem to be in special demand by people who dispense food, drink, and entertainment; the arms of the municipality add a certain cachet to bicycles, perambulators and wholesale consignments of tobacco; a tasteful miniature of the cathedral, or the Westgate, gives respectability to some commercial letterheads; the sorrow and anguish caused by the high price of suburban housing is sometimes mitigated by the pleasure of sporting an address evocative of archbishops, monasteries, or even Romans. For other purposes Elizabeth I, Falstaff and even poor little Agnes Wickfield, David Copperfield's girl friend, are pressed into service; and without going to the length of using a specific name, a trader may impart the right atmosphere by the use of the expression 'Ye Olde' followed by mock Chaucerian spelling, such as 'Canterburie Sausage Shoppe'. This prefix applied to The Beverley—I beg its pardon 'Beverlie'—public house at Hackington has actually resulted in its being entered under the letter 'Y' in the telephone book. (Or should we say 'Ye Olde Telephone Booke'). When will people learn that there never was an article 'ye', only a written abbreviation of 'the' based on the Saxon letter that stood for the 'th' sound?

Old customs continue. When senior aldermen address the city council as 'the Court', which it has not been since 1835, they are giving a practical example of the survival of folk memory. The city bounds are beaten—'When we can find time for it'. The council still smarting, possibly after 400 years, from Archbishop Parker's rebuke, processes in state to the cathedral on the great feast days of the church—Christmas, Eastertide and Whitsun, as well as on Remembrance Day, and other important occasions.

Many little ceremonies centre round Canterbury's surprising array of ancient almshouses. Under the will of Sir Roger Manwood, who died in 1592, the mayor has to visit annually the almshouses that Sir Roger founded, and which overlook St. Stephen's Green. The mayor must 'admonish' the brethren and sisters, and no doubt he pays some lip-service to this duty, but not so as to spoil appetites for the high tea that follows at The Beverley Inn.

Another Elizabethan lawyer of benevolent disposition was Sir John Boys who founded Jesus Hospital in Northgate. His half-timbered house in Palace Street is now the King's School shop.

There are some signs that interest in the past is growing; old habits are revived after centuries of disuse—the purple gown of the King's scholar, the white wand of the sheriff, the mayor's escort of Bluecoat (now Langton) boys. Even a new tradition may be maintained with the utmost tenacity. When The Buffs had their depot at Canterbury and there were regular soldiers at the barracks, every morning shortly before eleven o'clock the smartest private would march in full panoply of spotless blanco and gleaming boots from Howe Barracks down St. Martin's Hill to the cathedral to take part in a poignant ceremony; with the inherent dignity of complete impersonality and drilled precision of movement, the soldier would turn a page of the Book of Life, as the regiment's roll of honour is called; it is kept in the Warriors' Chapel in the south transept, where large numbers of visitors often watched the moving little ceremony. In the regular army, the term 'The Buffs' seems now to be little more than *part* of the title of a battalion which is *part* of the Queen's Regiment, but somehow the custom in the Warriors Chapel carries on; the country still has Territorial reservists and ex-soldiers to step into the breach when they are needed, and until the last part-time

Buff has been integrated out of existence the tradition, modern though it may be in origin, will be maintained.

Trace back the written word how far you will, and it will not tell of a time when Canterbury was not already ancient; medieval kings so described it in their charters. But it was not until Tudor and Stuart times that the antiquarian as such made his appearance. William Somner with his *Antiquities of Canterbury* (1640) was the first of a succession of learned men who have delved into the city's past, the history of its monuments and the contents of its archives. Nicholas Battely in 1703 carried on the story by revising Somner's book and publishing its second edition, and towards the end of the century Canon Gostling wrote his *Walk in and about Canterbury*; too old and shaky to leave his room to show his friends the things that he loved so well, he wished his book to act as a guide in his absence. The well-known eighteenth-century historian of Kent, Hasted, devoted two of his volumes to the city.

It was then the turn of archivists to take over the running from the general historian, and anyone who burrows into Canterbury's ancient documents, civic or ecclesiastical, is bound to come very quickly upon the name of Alderman Cyprian Bunce, librarian of the cathedral and honorary archivist of the city. With immense industry he ferreted, sorted, translated, and catalogued for the first time the Corporation's records; much of what he copied and digested from the archives he sent to the local press, which showed itself sufficiently enlightened not only to publish, but also to make off-prints of, the whole series. The alderman goes through the whole of the Burghmote minutes up to his own time (1800) and selects for reproduction the items that he obviously thinks will be of interest to the serious historian or student of social conditions; the sensational and the quaint find their place, but only as a *sauce piquante* to the main dish. We learn of the foundation of chantries, the coming of friars of various habit; the customs of trades; dimensions, measurements, and topography; and the vicissitudes of the Guildhall, and the various courts that sat there (these are minutely set out). Items of expenditure on food, drink and travel—claret at eightpence a gallon, with malmsey and 'ypochras' only a little more expensive, and such-like tantalising information—tell much of the economic conditions in Canterbury 400 years ago. In the sixteenth century rooms in London cost 1d. a night, and a slap-up dinner, wine included, 6d. Every time the king or queen is expected, the city fathers bestir themselves to purchase quantities of sand and gravel for the streets, a telling side-light on what must have been their normal condition. This expense, however was modest compared with that of the scented purse bulging with golden angels, or the silver-gilt cup brimful with coin that royalty expected as a normal present.

On the darker side, the account of the hanging and decapitation of 'Bluberd', the rebel hermit, heads a long list of executions for anything from theft or infanticide to high treason. A branding-iron for murderers cost 8d., while the disposal of a heretic was a more costly business; the bringing of the criminal from London, and the purchase of a load and a half of wood, sets the city back 14/8d. plus 8d. 'for the stake and staple'—ugh—'and 1d. for the gunpowder'. Some unlucky wretches certainly got to heaven the hard way.

Women's Lib. had yet to make headway in Canterbury. In 1520 a ducking-stool was provided, and fifty years later the sum of 9d. was incurred in 'writing papers for witches'; a mysterious activity connected perhaps with another entry of the same year— 'The grand jury present Mother Hudson of the parish of St. Mary Dungeon for that they vehemently suspect her to be a witch'. It was not easy to keep one's nose clean in those days, and the sheriff himself fell from grace; he was fined 3/4d. The offence? 'For wearing his beard'. Modern chancellors on the lookout for fresh sources of revenue might ponder this entry.

Vastly different from Bunce's selective but comprehensive extracts was Canterbury's contribution to the report of the Royal Commission on Historical Manuscripts in the 1880s. This came from the pen of Dr. Brigstock Sheppard. He gave a satisfactory account of the storage of the documents which were then in the room above the Westgate; many of the entries in them are set out *in extenso* in the original Latin, and no doubt Dr. Sheppard's was a scholarly excursus, even if not very informative to the ordinary reader.

It is Canterbury's shame that after the good old days, as recent as those of Brigstock Sheppard, there should have been disastrous damage to, and plundering of, the archives. How and by whom we have not yet been told, but clearly Mayor Francis Bennett-Goldney stands indicted for his very considerable and unscrupulous part in the catastrophe; for such it was. Goldney retrieved many of the documents from the cathedral library where they had been placed for safe custody; as honorary custodian of the Beaney museum he caused the bulk to be taken there and placed in an underground room, but the choicer items went to his own house, to remain there until after his death, when his executors were brought before the courts and compelled to disgorge the loot. Goldney's storage room at the Beaney was known only, it seems, to his own minions, and it was only after the Second World War that the cache was rediscovered, the door of the room having been hidden by accumulations of lumber. The place had been repeatedly flooded, and approximately ten per cent of the records were past saving; the percentage would have been greater but for a semi-miraculous feat of restoration on the part of the cathedral bookbinder, Mr. Maple.

Before Goldney, we know of no large-scale despoliation of the archives since the days of Wat Tyler in the fourteenth century; few parchments survived, as few prominent law-abiding men survived, Tyler's visit to Canterbury. After that, from sheer inertia as much as from any other cause, a vast mass of paper, parchment, sealing-wax, in bundles, rolls and scrolls; of indictment, presentment, recognisance, affidavit, taxation list, murage book, proclamation, petition and muster roll, together with massive books of minutes and accounts, accumulated as silt accumulates in a stagnant ditch. Even after the plundering and damage, a superb collection remains under the care of the present city archivist, who will deal firmly with any person or persons of ill-intent who might be disposed to emulate the depredations of Tyler or Goldney.

Alderman Bunce, in his printed extracts, had called mainly on the books, which are a small part only of the city archives. Some future Bunce may delve into the loose documents that make up their bulk; some of this work has already been done by the former archivist, Dr. William Urry, whose main task, however, was the immense one of rescue and classification. Whoever completes the work thus started is sure to reveal an entertaining catalogue of scandal and wrong-doing, and to open up new vistas on the social conditions of the last six hundred years.

One section of the records really cared for and not just casually collected is the splendid array of royal charters from the time of Henry II onwards. These conferred on the city its status and privileges, and under them Canterbury was governed until the Reform Act.

The charters are as magnificent in their way as Yevele's nave or the glass in Trinity Chapel. The first, issued about 1155 (it is not dated), is so beautifully written that a tyro (with only slight aid from a crib) can easily read it. Among the witnesses is one T. Cancs., which we are told stands for Thomas, Chancellor; Thomas Becket, no less. Most lawyers would hesitate to go into court and claim, on behalf of a citizen of Canterbury, the various rights and exemptions given to him by this charter. The citizens, it says, are to have their hunting wheresoever they held it in the time of King Henry I. Would the magistrates accept as a defence for trespassing in pursuit of game, that the defendant was a Canterbury citizen, and was only doing what had been done in King Henry's reign? The lucky citizens are also quit of brudtol, childwita, eresgieua and scotale. How would this go down in court as a defence to a claim for rates? (The first two, at any rate, sound as if they had something to do with broods of children, the care and education of whom figures so prominently in the rate-demand.)

Later charters have been mentioned in the story of Canterbury's climb to self-government—Henry III granted the city in fee farm, with power to elect its bailiffs; Henry VI instituted the mayoralty; and his supplanter, Edward IV, made the city a County, separate and distinct from the County of Kent *for ever*. The charters of Tudor and Stuart times, the constitutional heights having already been attained, dealt with internal regulation. They are remarkable, at the same time, for their illumination, which sometimes includes an excellent portrait of the monarch. Even more brilliantly decorated, with charming designs and pictures of animals, birds and flowers, as well as coats of arms, was the charter of James I issued in 1608.

Until a uniform and effective national system was developed in the nineteenth century, Canterbury had a well-used legal organisation of its own. The oldest court of all, the Burghmote, after developing an administrative arm ended by ceasing to be a court of law, though still called 'the Court'; the civil cases going to the Mayor's Court, or Court of Pleas. The Sessions took care of criminals, and both courts were underpinned by the whole panoply of medieval law-enforcement; Justices of the Peace,

King's School buildings from the Prior's Entry

Courts of Pie Powder, Sheriff's Court and the ancient court leet, or view of frankpledge.

For all the occasional irruptions, how peaceful is the world of the archivist compared with that of city government. We have always known that the king can do no wrong, and we now find out that the mayor can do no right. It is no use spending tens of thousands of pounds on restoring and repairing the city walls; more tens of thousands on pointing up the castle, repairing the Westgate, and mending the roof of the Poor Priests' Hospital; this will buy you no credit in the harsh world of environmental criticism. 'City survived the war, but hasn't survived the peace', is about all the thanks you will get, which is hardly encouraging.

One thing that Mr. Mayor will never lack is plenty of advice. This is largely dispensed by amenity societies, of necessity talkers rather than doers, prolific in ideal schemes, but less effective in balancing the ideal against the facts of life, practical, administrative, and financial. They are also, as a rule, less than perfect in 'identifying'—a vogue word in those circles—the elusive boundary between restoration and faking, between maintaining an ancient building and fabricating a new dummy. To see the difficulty, and perhaps to understand why the criticisms and offers of advice have not helped very much in tackling the problem, one has only to look at the different histories of the cathedral and the medieval Guildhall.

The Caen stone of the cathedral is so soft that if nothing is done in the course of centuries it will simply weather away; first the outer surface will go, and with it all traces of any mouldings, carvings and other modelling; then, if left long enough, the stone will disintegrate completely and the building may fall down. For this reason, repair work and replacement of damaged and worn-out stone is almost continuous, and we have to accept the certainty that in course of time the whole outer skin will be renewed, so that what people see will not be the original material at all. Common sense tells us that no argument is needed to justify this repair process, which the Dean and Chapter carry out at such great expense; in fact they must be congratulated on the job that they do.

By contrast, it is clear that to have tried to preserve as a medieval building the Guildhall, after it showed signs of collapse in 1950, would have resulted in nothing but, to use Dr.

Two views of the River Stour and the Westgate Gardens

Holden's phrase, 'a picturesque dummy'. The dire effects of five centuries of natural decay had been made worse by unskilled alterations at different times in the building's history which had mutilated its fabric. The beams that had once supported the roof, but had now ceased to do so, were rotten, and the flint walls quickly disintegrated into loose stone and powder when probed gently to test their stability. The result of all this was that before reconstruction could be started, the builders would have had to pull down the superstructure to within four feet of the ground; and only a small fraction of the old material could have been built into the new work. Considerable expense could not be justified unless the building could be made capable of some modern use; and the final appearance and design would have had little resemblance, if any, to the original.

One of the principal uses of the Guildhall, as a magistrates' court, was ruled out when their worships announced that never again would they return to it, so cramped and inadequate did they consider it to be. In short, the cost of rebuilding would have been enormous, the usefulness of the resulting building negligible, and the structure itself no genuine restoration but a new building, with at the best a certain amount of old material incorporated.

So, with central government concurrence, the building had to go, the vaults and pillars of an earlier structure in the basement being preserved. The decision was painful but inescapable; yet to this day conservationists rake up the affair, and speak of the callous 'tearing down' of the ancient Guildhall as if those responsible had, for motives of their own, destroyed a perfectly satisfactory building.

We go back to the critic who thought that Canterbury had survived the war 'fairly intact'. By implication he includes it in his general indictment of cathedral cities where there are narrow streets choked with heavy traffic, indiscriminate widening of roads, and a rash of shops and stores with no individuality; where there is belief in supermarkets, the motor-car, and nice wide streets, 'and if a few historic towns are destroyed in the process—too bad, but this is progress'.

For Canterbury, this typical denunciation side-steps the serious problem that Reichsmarschall Goering left when he blotted out those 800 buildings and seriously damaged another 1,000, by simply ignoring it. An old building can be preserved, but no one can *build* an old building, and the same goes for an old area. Do the critics think, perhaps, that the new should masquerade as old? If so they will run into the equally vocal body of counter-criticism that sarcastically denounces reproduction architecture. Are we to have Queen Anne fronts and Mary Anne backs? Is the treatment to be veneer-ial? Or perhaps 'contemptuary'?— with Cotswold stone landscaping of the traffic islands, and such-like 'God-wottery'?

Canterbury rejected these gimmicks, and its reconstruction, whether successful or unsuccessful, was a straightforward and honest attempt (with the help of, amongst others, three past or future Presidents of the Royal Institute of British Architects and of the Royal Fine Art Commission), to restore to life the blasted waste of the bombed area.

Whatever the conservationists may say, the eternal character of an ancient but thriving city, even if it suffers no sudden calamities, is one of gradual but inevitable change, a process that gives such a place its special flavour and charm.

Finally, do not believe that what you read about Canterbury in a newspaper, however eminent, is the whole story. Fleet Street, when it is so minded, can give a false impression without printing a single word that is not strictly true—by the simple device of reporting one side only of the case. When for example the city council wished to build a car-park that some people did not like, the conservationist bandwaggon started to roll and a certain national newspaper printed columns of bitter criticism and denunciation for many days. But when, after a high-level conference, at which the Minister himself and three other members of the government were present, a press statement was issued clearing the city council of many of the imputations made against them, the affair seemed suddenly to lose its news value; and if a report of the Minister's press statement ever appeared in the national newspaper, we in Canterbury have yet to see it.

On matters environmental, criticism or denunciation of the city council are news; their rebuttal, even on the authority of a Minister of the Crown, is not.

SISTER MARY CLARE

The peaceful and unexciting story of the re-establishment of the Roman Catholic Church in Canterbury contrasts with the wild eventful saga of the Hales family, and their efforts to keep the flag of that religion flying in the city; a saga which involved a lawsuit that made constitutional history, followed closely by the death of the son of the house in the Battle of the Boyne, and ended when the last of the family estates were sold by the mortgagees of a Carmelite nun. Ended? Or merely given new character?

The purchasers were the Jesuits; expelled from the land from which they had induced Louis XIV to drive out the Huguenots, they now themselves sought refuge in—or at least near—the very city that had succoured their victims. The wheel had indeed turned full circle.

The Hales family had come to Canterbury in the seventeenth century. Already wealthy, the grandson of the first baronet married Lady Wotton and so added the large St. Augustine's estate to the family possessions at St. Stephen's, then just outside and now within the city.

It was not until 1685 that the third Edward Hales formally declared himself a Roman Catholic; he thought he had discovered a way of driving a coach-and-horses through the anti-Catholic Test Act by taking advantage of the dispensing power of the Crown. Edward defied the Act, openly committed breaches of it, induced his own coachman, one Godden, to prosecute him, and then obtained from the sympathetic James II a dispensation for his offences which he produced at the trial, and which the judges of the King's Bench accepted as valid. This was the celebrated constitutional law case of *Godden v. Hales*, that students learn about to this day. They are also taught that in the Bill of Rights, that Parliament soon passed, the action of King James was declared illegal.

The ingenious Sir Edward bought the former mansion of Sir Roger Manwood, the Elizabethan judge who established the almshouses that still overlook St. Stephen's Green, and whose tomb is in the parish church. Canterbury was not very worried about the Catholicism of the Hales so long as they continued their series of public-spirited acts in presenting the citizens with various useful assets, such as a water supply. The undoing of the family was due not to their religion but to their improvidence; they built, about 1758, an enormous Doric-style mansion which exhausted the family bank-account and loaded its members with debts and mortgages.

The sad day came when the last Edward Hales died leaving no son, and an only daughter who had already taken as a nun vows of perpetual poverty and chastity. The Hales had French connections, and the Carmelite Sister Mary Clare was born in Boulogne, though baptised in Canterbury as Barbara Mary Felicity. The vow of poverty requires Carmelites, if they inherit wealth, to disclaim it, and it looked certain that the Hales Place estate would go to the French branch of the family, named de Morlaincourt; the legal documents were drawn up and taken to France for the pious nun to sign. But something went wrong; overcome perhaps by the finality and the solemnity of the step she was about to take, Sister Mary Clare sought the advice of the English solicitor's clerk who had come to get her signature.

'I wouldn't sign, if it were me,' said the honest fellow.

'But what will my prioress have to say if I don't?'

'You needn't be in any hurry to tell her; think what you could do with the money.'

Mary Clare's eyes started to shine. 'What could I not do! For my Order. Why not another Carmel at Hales' Place?'

'Why not?' said the clerk. 'I take it then that you won't be wanting these documents?' and he put them back in his satchel.

Alas, even the most worthy schemes can go wrong; the new Carmel was started, but never rose more than a few feet above the ground; its last vestiges were swept away when the Hales' Place housing estate was developed after the Second World War.

In fact, Mary Clare's project reacted upon its innocent sponsor by drawing the attention of the Roman Catholic hierarchy to what was going on, and especially to the affair of the unsigned documents. Chaperoned by a Benedictine monk, Sister Mary Clare was summoned to Rome where, having been kept in ignorance of the purpose of her journey, she was dismayed to learn that the vows of obedience and poverty were inconsistent with the position of a hereditary landowner. The Holy Father himself, Pio Nono, gently chided the errant but well-meaning Carmelite, insisted on a forced dispensation of the vows, excepting, at Mary Clare's request, that of chastity, and soothed her ruffled feelings by the accord of numerous liturgical privileges and the gift of a piece of the True Cross.

It is a sad reflection that given a little more time Miss Hales would have ceased to be in conflict with her vows. Immoderately generous, extravagant to a degree, and possessed by a taste for costly antiques, she soon ran through what money was left, and mortgagees took over the estate.

It was at this juncture that the fugitive Jesuits purchased the mansion, which their community retained until the 1920s, when La Belle France allowed them to return. But no one could be found to run the mansion, or maintain it, and in 1928 it was pulled down. Poor Mary Clare had died, many years before, at Sarre Court in Thanet, in dire poverty after all.

The Hales Place estate was, many years ago, cut up for modern housing. The 'drive' that led to the mansion and the 'terrace' on which it fronted have long ago been given capital letters, and had their roadways made up under the Private Streetworks Act. From the terrace a woodland walk, directing its view on to Bell Harry, led to a walled pleasance; some part of this landscape-gardening remains today as a tangled wilderness, a no-man's-land between private and council houses. At the edge of this little jungle, a short way from the new community centre, rises a tight ring of thirteen enormously tall limes. In the midst of this ring is a tiny round chapel built of flint, brick, stone, and human bones; between the little chapel and the 100-foot-high trees is an inner circle of graves, and beyond the trees, an outer one, the whole surrounded by a ring fence of broken wire, thorn and bramble. Children have smashed down the headstones, but the inscriptions show that in this forlorn place were buried Jesuits with French names, at dates from the 1880s to the 1920s. This neglected little cemetery is the last memorial of the Jesuits of Canterbury, and indirectly of the Hales family, of Sister Mary Clare, and of Canterbury's connection with *Godden v. Hales*, the Battle of the Boyne and the Bill of Rights. Its unseemly state is a reproach to the city.

ELEVEN

FÊTES CHAMPÊTRES

SPRING will come quite suddenly to Canterbury, catching her almost unawares; in one magic instant the place is transformed. To brood on the happenings of centuries ago, on martyrdoms, stern conflicts and painful struggles, to worry about the irritating present or the uncertain future is to dwell on unreal trifles that are best, for these golden moments, forgotten. Let all be happy.

All around the city is the Garden of England, and the whole landscape of the rolling downland is in a pinky-white pastel haze of blossom, a shortlived spectacle, giving many a citizen a guilty feeling that he has let this fairy-like vision slip away before he has made the time to enjoy it. The blossom falls, and the young fruit sets as nature's annual transformation-scene of bud and branch unfolds, fading from black to brown, from brown to yellow, from yellow to pale and then to brightest green, in woodland, copse and hedgerow, as the hops climb higher. There are days of storm and days of rain, rain that washes the air so clean that when the warm sun does appear he rides in a sky of Mediterranean blue, pouring his rays through a crystal atmosphere. Then indeed does the magic of Canterbury bewitch its mortal inhabitants. The River Stour, from being a turbulent, overcharged and muddy torrent watched with apprehension by the River Authority and by bankside householders, resumes its good behaviour, with peaceful and pellucid waters alive with trout and other less glamorous fish, so that there can be boating down at Westgate, fishing, legal and illegal in sundry spots, and the launching of canoes and kyacks at the Long Bridge near Kingsmead.

Easter sees the first influx of happy day-trippers, and there are more still at Whitsuntide. Then in June comes the first great event in the Canterbury season, the Festival of the Friends of the

Cathedral. It is less ambitious today than in the '30s and '40s when Margaret Babington was commissioning such writers as John Masefield, Laurence Binyon, T. S. Eliot, Dorothy Sayers, Christopher Fry, Robert Gittings and Christopher Hassall to write plays for it. There will perhaps never again be discovered among the commissioned works such a world masterpiece as *Murder in the Cathedral*, first performed in 1935; but it was not the only Festival play to be seen or heard by a much wider audience. Several others had this distinction through performances later in the commercial theatre and the studios of the B.B.C.; indeed a movement towards a Christian drama of the twentieth century was born in those heroic years, and it must surely not be allowed to die.

As the Friends hold their Festival there comes the season of flowers, when the city's greenhouses triumphantly disgorge enormous numbers of summer plants to replace the fading tulips and wallflowers. From post and transom hang the baskets trailing tendrils of colour, the familiar geraniums and petunias varied by many other colourful and exotic blooms whose names are known only to the keen gardener or the botanist.

Behind the pubs grass pitches are mown and rolled, for not satisfied with its ample installations for playing all the normal English games, outdoor and indoor, the city has its own special local pastime known as 'bat and trap'.

The bat is a short, thick one, shaped like that used for table tennis, but heavier; the trap an oblong wooden box with a loose piece of wood on top; the ball is of hard rubber, and the outdoor pitches are in the back gardens of sundry public houses. There is some resemblance to cricket, but it is a very loose one; there is a batting side and a fielding side. The game is played in this wise: The batsman puts the ball on the trap, taps the loose piece of wood so that the ball jumps in the air, and tries to hit it between two goalposts behind which the fielding side is congregated, at the other end of the pitch; if he fails he is out, but if he succeeds, he scores a run. One of the fielders is then allowed to bowl the ball along the ground at a little target fixed at the front end of the trap. The unfortunate batsman is given no chance to defend his wicket, but must stand helpless, and hope that the unskilfulness of the bowler, or the bumpiness of the ground, will preserve his wicket, for if the target is knocked down, he is out. This is a real, good-neighbourly, good-humoured, public house team-game, lending itself to great hilarity and shouting. The exertions on a warm summer's evening stimulate a demand for copious draughts of ale, from which the degree of skill required does not seem to enjoin abstinence.

Summer reaches its height before the peak of the tourist mass-invasion, and Canterbury is now at its best. The balmy evenings are long, the roses are ablaze in the riverside gardens at Westgate, where nenuphars crowd the rock-pools, and the gouty walnut tree of great but unknown age signposts the shady waterside path bordered by giant weeping willows. And these Elysian fields are sheltered from commerce and motor-cars by the mass of the Gate itself, which makes with Holy Cross Church in the foreground and a delicate screen of flowering trees, a romantic subject for the tourist's camera. Across the river, half-timbered Tudor cottages keep the illusion that this is Merry England, and not the computerised, car-ridden Britain of the seventies.

A bare half-a-mile from Westgate are the gardens called 'Dane John', that essentially Canterbury name, a corruption of the Norman donjon (like dungeon) and nothing to do with Danes. Here the Roman wall angles round the prehistoric mound—fortunately we are done with history now, except perhaps that of games and pastimes, so need not say anything about how pre-historic it is or why it is there at all—and here Marlowe's little Muse now stands, as does the Invicta locomotive from the old Canterbury–Whitstable railway. What exactly the Dane John comprises no one is quite sure; whether it just means the gardens, or if the term includes the Municipal Offices and the terraces of Regency houses that look on to it, is a moot point. However that may be, here is a place where mums and dads can relax and bask in the hot sun, with the shade of the lime trees at hand if they want to move into it, while their offspring can also sit and rest or, as is more likely, infringe the byelaws by playing football, running on the flower beds and sliding down the slopes of the Mound and the ramps of the city walls.

As summer advances, the time comes for the Green Court in the Precincts to render its annual tribute to education and the social round; in July comes King's Week, which means orchestras in the cathedral, drama in the Shirley Hall, string serenades in the cloisters and *A Midsummer Night's Dream* in the Archdeacon's garden, and as a climax a glorious jamboree, when prizes are distributed and speeches made, and teas and ices are dispersed from marquees on the Green Court for parents, staff and other guests.

It is now late in July; the King's School boys and their tuck boxes will be going home, and in a few more days the action will switch to yet another pleasant greensward, in south Canterbury, the St. Lawrence Cricket Ground. In August there comes, as it has come for 130 years with wartime gaps, that best known and best loved of all cricket festivals, Canterbury Week. The city is the home of Kent cricket, and thereby hangs a long and interesting story told for amusement only, and not to bolster claims of 'first ever', 'oldest', 'greatest' or other use of superlatives.

Cricket, says Dr. Johnson, is a sport at which the contenders drive a ball with sticks in opposition to one another; and the game was at one time or another confused with polo, golf, tipcat, cat-and-dog and stoolball; but in Canterbury cricket has been cricket for quite a time. 'The City,' said Lord Harris, the famous Kent player, 'long being the headquarters of the game in the county is justly entitled to be regarded as the home of Kent cricket'. Now, Kent cricket, along perhaps with London cricket, is the oldest in the world. If you say this, many people start talking about Hampshire and Hambledon. Stuff and nonsense! They came much later. Why, even in the seventeenth century Sunday cricket was one of the seven deadly sins which scandalised a Puritan divine at Maidstone; which shows that Canterbury though now the home, was not the cradle of Kent cricket. Apart from Maidstone's anticipation of the John Player League, when did reasonably organised and reasonably lawful cricket start—county cricket matches for instance? Well, the answer is (as has been said, as a matter of interest only) that the first county match on record was played in 1719 between Kent and London (identical then with Middlesex). And the first match of which the score has been preserved is Kent v. All England, 18th June 1744, when Kent won by one wicket. This was one of the great periods of Kent cricket, when they were styled 'the unconquerable county'. An exaggeration, because in the return match at Canterbury, Kent lost.

In the 1840s cricket was dominated by a remarkable man named Fuller Pilch, the Don Bradman of those times. Although he was born in Norfolk, Kent signed him up and persuaded him to go and live at Malling, so that he could play for the county. Then, in

1842, Canterbury became their headquarters, and Pilch removed to the city and, incidentally, became the licensee of The Saracen's Head. The annual Cricket Week also dates from the arrival of Fuller Pilch who, a new St. Augustine, put Canterbury on the cricket as well as on the religious map.

On Pilch's gravestone in St. Gregory's churchyard can be seen a bas-relief of the great batsman at the wicket. Older books say that he is shown having been bowled middle-stump by bowler Death, but on inspection, we notice that the wicket is intact. Quite obviously Fuller, with the kind assistance perhaps of the County Committee, is taking his second innings, and so far has kept the ball out of his stumps.

With the establishment of the Cricket Week was linked the formation of the Old Stagers, when two 'County' types, Mr. John Baker and the Hon. Frederick Ponsonby, with the help of a number of Cambridge men, hit on the idea of amateur theatricals to amuse visitors to the cricket festival after the close of play each evening. The Old Stagers have their own special customs, traditions, and 'in' jokes—their affinity to I Zingari and the Band of Brothers, and the rule that every performer not a member of a certain club is one of 'the Smith family'. Both Arthur Sullivan and W. S. Gilbert have been 'Smiths' in their time, as have a host of distinguished actors and actresses. On the stage of the Marlowe Theatre the Old Stagers are still going strong after 130 years.

It was five years after their move to Canterbury that the Kent Club secured the St. Lawrence Ground (named after a long-disappeared leper hospital) and moved there lock, stock and barrel. Their Canterbury matches, and the famous Week have been held there ever since.

Kent cricket has a glorious history, and is esteemed no less for its tradition of sportsmanship than for its many past victories. Pre-eminent in the 1740s and again in the 1840s, Kent had another revival of fortune in the 1900s, and have in recent years again tasted success in the Championship and also in one-day cricket, which has proved to be definitely to the liking of the dashing type of Kent sportsman.

The story of Kent cricket is indeed one of far-fetched yarns, humour, triumph and disaster. In the old days there was sometimes complaint about the state of the outfield, and even the infield, and it was once reported that a brace of partridges was got between point and wicket after several overs had been bowled. On other occasions, rabbits and birds are reported as having been killed by the ball.

Kent suffered a shocking and humiliating disaster during Canterbury Week in 1862. In the ranks of the visiting team a mystery-man was detected whose participation represented a grave threat to Kent, because his name was E. M. Grace. At first the Kent team refused to play unless Grace, whom they considered to be unqualified, was dropped. When it was pointed out that they would have to give all the spectators their money back if the match did not take place Kent agreed, grumblingly, to continue. They were thoroughly trounced, as the interloper followed an innings of 192 not out with the capture of all ten wickets in Kent's second innings. But this was not the worst; one of the umpires was none other than the celebrated Fuller Pilch, and after the match Pilch admitted that he had given Grace not out when he was clearly caught at the wicket because Pilch wanted to see the great man in action.

Such is the story. Lord Harris doubts its complete truth, but it is a good one for all that. Contrast this woeful episode with the gladsome events of 1884 when the first county caps, embroidered with the white horse of Kent, were presented to the Gentlemen in the team. Well had they earned them, for they had beaten the Australians.

Yorkshiremen will be interested to know that it was a famous Kent player, Charles Inglis Thornton, who originated the Scarborough Cricket Festival. It is claimed that Thornton was the greatest hitter the world has ever seen, and impressive statistics are given of the enormous lengths of the various hits he made, and of the number of runs that were taken while the ball was on the way up to and down from the heavens.

There was more 'Grace' trouble in 1876 at Canterbury when 'W.G.' scored a record 344 for the M.C.C. However, the County survived, and in 1906 for the first time since the modern competition was established they won the Championship. In 1909 they were champions again, and in 1910 and 1913. Further success did not come again for another fifty-seven years, but before the 1970 triumph, Kent had won the Gillette Cup Knockout competition in 1967.

The wait for championship honours was enlivened by the performances of some of the world's greatest cricketers whom the county produced; not only great but always entertaining, force-ful batsmen, agile wicket-keepers, cunning bowlers with characteristic styles. The dashing Kent Cavalier, whom the more sober-sided had to restrain when there was that little trouble with the Roundheads, has indeed come into his own in Kent cricket.

Lord Harris described the Canterbury Week as the Goodwood of Cricket, and although the games are serious championship matches, the general atmosphere is one of gaiety and festivity. One side of the ground is taken up by the marquees of different personalities, clubs, clans and groups, from the President of the Kent Club to the Mayor of Canterbury, from the Band of Brothers to the Chamber of Trade. Today there is some attempt to decorate the city, not very happily, with strings of bunting, which reminds one rather of a small French village *en fête*, and more worthily by floodlighting the cathedral, ancient buildings and riverside vistas, with sometimes *Son et Lumière* in the Green Court as well. Apart from the floodlighting it was even gayer sixty years ago with, in the evening, fashionable johnnies strolling about the streets in evening dress because of the limited sitting-out facilities in local ball-rooms.

Thursday is Ladies' Day, the most fashionable one socially; if you think you are somebody you must be seen at St. Lawrence on that day. Except for the sacred pitch itself the whole ground (when the contenders are not driving the ball in opposition to one another) is a place for strolling and gossip; then the bell rings and the umpires amble out, their leisurely progress giving the crowds time to disperse; finally, when all is clear, out come the white-clad figures and the serious business of the day resumes. It is usually very sedate, but you never know; suddenly the game may catch fire. The spectators may have waited hours, even days, but when this happens—say Kent, facing a big score, short of time, decide to go for the runs and get on top—what fireworks! What fever of excitement! The opposition quite demoralised; the scoreboard figures whirling frienziedly to keep up with the stream of fours and sixes; then to a shout that can be heard in the Dane John, the winning hit, and pandemonium. Good Old Kent! When this happens it makes worth while the hours of blocking and prodding that the crowds may have watched. And, happy thought, no bungling government, no bureaucrat, nay, not even any trade union mandarin dare put a hand on this. Not on Canterbury Week!

The Canterbury Cricket Week is rather like Christmas, which comes round every year yet never seems to lose its appeal; life would be unthinkable for the Men of Kent and many others without it.

There is another kind of celebration, which may be solemn and commemorative or light-hearted and apropos of nothing in particular, that will be enriched by atmosphere and background and tradition in Canterbury as nowhere else. The city's part in the Festival of Britain was one example, and its Coronation celebrations two years later another; the 800th anniversary of the death of Becket in 1970 a third. Those who saw these events, and even more those who took part in them, have memories that they will keep all their lives.

The Festival Exhibition that was so actual, with its real Roman and medieval remains, real bomb damage, real hops and apple trees (for there was still an orchard behind the buildings in St. George's Street before they were destroyed) and actual recordings of air-raids noises, made people feel that they were really taking part in hundreds of years of history. The pageant-play of St. Augustine's with its pathetic scenes of despoliation and the triumphant return of the ghosts of the past to see its rebirth as St. Augustine's College, all enacted amid the stones of the old monastery, brought lumps to people's throats; and the Coronation celebrations, when the main A28 road was blocked for days and converted into an auditorium for the display of fireworks, torchlight processions and the pageantry of the kings, queens and emperors who had trodden the streets of Canterbury in the last couple of thousand years, put patriotism into the perspective of history.

Such events do not generate a mere passing enthusiasm or sentimentality, but serve rather to awake the joy of artistic achievement, genuine pride in one's native or adoptive city, and regard for one's fellow citizens that is scarcely conceivable outside the ambience of Canterbury.

The Becket commemoration brought Pontifical Mass, after 400 years, to the precincts of Canterbury Cathedral. The mixing with Protestant pageantry of the splendid pomp of the Catholic hierarchy and its multi-coloured uniformed orders, the shared worship and the exchanges of hospitality, not merely symbolised the desire for reconciliation but actually engendered, in the unique setting of Canterbury, a spirit of friendship and mutual respect.

As spring advances, not only the pilgrims but Canterburians too, will be seen making for the coast in their cars, or perhaps slipping away to the nearest yacht club, donning jodhpurs, getting out their fishing tackle—fresh-water or sea—or just driving out into the country. There is no place so attractive that beautiful and interesting surroundings will not make it more so, and Canterbury lies folded in the North Downs which, in the pompous phraseology of Whitehall, are an area of outstanding natural beauty. East Kent as a whole is a richly historic region where Roman and pre-Roman sites abound, where ancient Cinque Ports line the coast, and equally ancient villages are dotted about the highways and byways. The sea is all round Canterbury, and the non-native always seems surprised to hear that to the north it is within six miles.

And Dover, gateway to all the delights of the Continent, and gateway also for the Continentals to the delights of Kent and the bargains of Messrs. 'Marks and Spensair' is to the south-east, a mere fifteen miles (or twenty-four kilometres) along the Roman road.

Within fifteen miles too are many other attractions, for while the landscape of East Kent may not have the majesty of the Scottish Highlands, or the windswept grandeur of the Pennine Moors, it does possess a cosy picturesqueness of its own, and a network of narrow lanes that go on for mile after mile leading to nowhere in particular.

The Hastings road threads its way through the pleasant defile that the River Stour made through the barrier of the downs, touching interesting little places en route. Chartham has a huge mill that specialises in the manufacture of tracing paper so flawless that for some purposes it is the only source of supply in the whole world. A paper-mill scarcely fits in with the conception of outstanding natural beauty, but the ancient church redeems the village, and its Septvans funerary brass attracts brass-rubbers from far and wide. A few miles further on the route skirts Chilham, a village of character, possessing a fine square, a well-known lived-in castle, some parts of which are medieval, a heronry, and the grave of a mythical giant, Julliberrie, really a long barrow. The Kentish novelist, R. Austin Freeman, used it as a setting for one of Dr. Thorndyke's exploits. At Godmersham is the country seat that appears in Jane Austen's works as Mansfield House. The old market town of Wye has a racecourse and an agricultural college, equally well known. Beyond expanding industrial Ashford the road meanders on into the Weald of Kent, through Tenterden, near which Caxton was born, and at last out of the county into Sussex.

Diverging at no great angle from the Ashford road is Stone Street, a Roman road going due south in the direction of Roman Lemanis, modern Lympne (pronounced Lim), a small change of direction, but a large change in character. Instead of following the meanderings of a valley, Stone Street runs almost dead straight and, once it reaches the 400-foot contour of the downland plateau, almost dead flat. For over twelve miles there is no village, only isolated farms and cottages. After riding the top of the escarpment, whence the view extends to the nuclear power station on Dungeness and to the distant mass of Beachy Head, the road makes a curving traverse descent; thence, after running through the village of Stanford and by Folkestone Racecourse, Stone Street decants you at a meeting of roads, where you have the choice of going to Folkestone, Hythe or Ashford, to the cross-Channel airport at Lympne, or the one at Lydd, to the Romney, Hythe and Dymchurch Railway, the smallest commercially operated one in the world, or in summer to swim at Dymchurch or picnic among the sheep on Romney Marsh.

Other roads, some busy, some quiet, some pretty and some not, radiate from Canterbury to all points of the compass; the Ashford road and Stone Street are fairly typical. Fordwich, as a former borough, still has its Lilliputian town hall and its ducking stool; it is a mere two or three miles away down the Stour, just off the Margate road. Other destinations surround the city, like the figures on a clock; at ten o'clock is Faversham, half industrialised, half old, boasting a town hall on stilts, a street of ancient houses devotedly restored, and a creek that for some reason is something of a joke; at eleven or half-past are Whitstable and the oyster beds; at one o'clock, Herne Bay and its second-longest English pier. The imaginary afternoon wears on with Reculver, twin Roman fort to Richborough, guarding the Wantsum channel, Westgate, Margate, Ted Heath's home town of Broadstairs, Ramsgate, Pegwell Bay, where the Saxons possibly did (and the hovercraft certainly do) land. For Sandwich, at three o'clock, Canterbury people have a great love, for it is really a pocket edition of their city, and senior of the Cinque Ports. The two great golf courses, Royal St. George's and Prince's, are a trifle too

The Barton Court School

swanky for most Canterburian players of the great game. They seem to feel more at home (when they want a change from their own course at Scotland Hills) at the Royal Cinque Ports at Deal; the town has a Regency sea-front and, if you count the head-quarters of the Lord Warden at Walmer and the ruins of Sandown, three Tudor castles.

Once in a while Canterbury people visit St. Margaret's Bay, nestling against the South Foreland and well off the beaten track; though not so far off as before the war, when it was a quiet retreat for the wealthy and famous. During the conflict, com-mando training in street fighting was made more realistic by the intermittent arrival of German shells from Sangatte, and the old St. Margaret's Bay is no more.

Beyond the South Foreland, Dover and Folkestone need no introduction. The port of Dover brings Canterbury to within thirty-seven miles by road and sea of Calais—about the same distance as Dartford in the other direction. Hustlers can make the 'Med' in twenty-four hours flat, while the middle-aged, or those plodding along impeded by caravan, can be in Turin within forty-eight, door to door.

Who living in delectable Canterbury wants to go to Calais, the Mediterranean or Turin? To live idyllically and still go away for holidays is wanting to have things both ways.

Well, who doesn't?

The reputation of Canterbury abroad is, if anything, greater than in England. Functionaries beam when they see the name of the city on the *fiche*, important towns such as Rheims seek Canterbury's friendship; *Murder in the Cathedral* is performed in Naples; films of *The Canterbury Tales* are exhibited in remote parts of Apulia, with a reminder that obscenity is in the mind of the beholder. Even a Jewish lawyer from Brooklyn has heard, in Toity-toid Street, of the 'place where some cardinal fellow got knocked on the head'.

Reims, Firenze, Salzburg, they are the league that Canterbury bats in abroad; in England the city seems to be appreciated best by other towns with similar traditions. (The contempt of the industrial ant-heaps of the north and midlands for a city of only thirty-odd thousand inhabitants is bottomless.)

In one corner of the city's portrait is a kind of blur composed of Egham, Runnymede, Windsor, St. Alban's, Bury St. Edmunds,

12

The Cathedral, floodlit

London, Master of the Rolls, American Bar Association, with a glimpse of a boat to be pushed out every fifteen years when Canterbury's turn comes round; this is the Magna Carta business, for Canterbury is in the Magna Carta Trust, a sort of league for keeping the memory of King John, the barons and the Charter before the public, British and American.

Though not institutionally, yet by facts ancient and modern, Canterbury and Oxford are manifoldly linked. In 1362 Archbishop Islip founded Canterbury College at Oxford, to train clerks for Christchurch. Henry VIII dissolved the college as he dissolved the monastery, but its name is perpetuated by Canterbury Quad. Is it only a coincidence that the college that Cardinal Wolsey founded on virtually the same spot was also named Christ Church?

The tomb of Archbishop Chichele and its link with All Souls we have already heard about; the same connection has resulted in the south-west tower of Canterbury Cathedral, built while Chichele was archbishop, being known as 'the Oxford steeple'.

Both cities have claimed the first Franciscan settlement in England—certainly it was one and the same expedition that founded the friaries in both places.

For much of what we know about Roman and mediaeval Canterbury we are indebted to scholars who have ended their academic odysseys at Oxford University. Professor Sheppard Frere, of All Souls, who directed most of the excavations in the blitzed areas, is now the university's Professor of the Archaeology of the Roman Empire, and Dr. William Urry, of St. Edmund Hall, formerly the city and cathedral archivist, author of *Canterbury under the Angevin Kings*, is Oxford's Reader in Medieval Palaeography.

And perhaps the most intriguing link of all; after many of the most expert planners in the world had been baffled by the Oxford Road Plan problem, and the famous controversy about the road across Christ Church Meadows, it was to Canterbury's former Planning Officer, Sir Hugh Wilson, that Oxford turned for final guidance. And got it too.

TWELVE

POSTSCRIPT

SUCH then, as seen through the eyes of one person, is the portrait of Canterbury. As we take the work to be, as it were, varnished and framed, we leave the city poised, as so often before, between hope and apprehension.

The Canterburian daunted by the uncertainties, can go where strength and inspiration are to be found, and his way is through the ancient gateway into the Precincts. He who goes in, even if it is for the thousandth time, finds himself straightway in another world; time can never take away the sense of peace or the over-powering impression of grandeur of the cathedral seen from near at hand.

Memory recalls the great occasions; the Primate entering in pontifical state with crozier and mitre, and later seen standing before the metropolitical throne, beaming at the congregation. The two angelic—for the moment at least—cherubs who have carried his train nestle before him, and the cross of Canterbury is on its stand.

Recalled, too, are the magnificent popular services, often with a military element, so that the band of The Buffs, or what is left of them, are ranged in tiers on the steps that lead up to the choir, for once in surroundings where the loudest, the most strident notes are mellowed and softened by the vastnesses aloft and around.

It is comforting, in the gathering gloom of some weary winter afternoon, to go to the great church. Whether for effect, or perhaps for the sake of economy, some only of the lamps are burning within. In the nave, the roof-vaulting high above is suffused in golden radiance, a joy to the upturned eye, but shedding only a thin gleam ninety feet below, so that the vault seems to float ethereally.

In the choir it is even darker. There is just enough of the day left to strike, here and there, a dull ember of colour from the deepening opacity of the stained glass. By some chance, a bright pool of light falls on the worn steps of the aisle curving up through the shadowed grille to Trinity Chapel. Beyond loom the vague outlines of a royal tomb and of darkling pillars. This accidental composition, to which Anselm, William of Sens, an unknown tomb-designer, and the Dean's electricians have contributed, is somehow symbolic and comforting.

Outside, indifference may neglect, weakness may endanger, and folly may destroy the landmarks of sanity and tradition, but in here nothing is going to change very much.

Not for a long, long time.

LOCAL GOVERNMENT

By the time these words are read the present City of Canterbury will have ceased to exist. It was so enacted in the Conservative Government's Local Government Act, of 1972. The former city will now be ruled by a District Council in which Canterbury will be combined with Whitstable and Herne Bay, and with the surrounding and intermediate rural area that goes under the name of Bridge-Blean.

Although it will have three times the population of the present city, the new District will have some only of the powers that the city now has, and practically none of the important ones; these all have gone to the Kent County Council (which is bad enough), or worse still, to the central government and the civil servants.

How has this happened? Has the ancient city completely fallen down on the job? Has it not fought hard enough to keep its identity? Short of starting another Peasants' Revolt, marching up to London, and chopping off the heads of a few unpopular ministers (a course that would undoubtedly have had its attractions) it is hard to say what more the city could have done.

We have seen from the careers of people like Nicholas Faunt and John Twyne how difficult it was at times for local leaders to keep on the right side of kings and queens, but Canterbury managed to do this in the long run and secured the status of a county of a city, appointing its own sheriff, and being made separate and distinct from the County of Kent *for ever*. In 1888 when county councils were started, again Canterbury managed to keep out of Kent, being created a county borough. Since that time all its efforts have been devoted to keeping that status, no easy matter in the light of the small population—about half that of the next smallest county borough. To avoid any possible accusation of mismanagement, when modern conditions required a large organisation for administering, say, the police or the fire brigade, Canterbury compromised and made a deal with the County Council for joint working arrangements. For the largest, costliest and most important local government service, education, the city again made a composition with Kent, but of a different kind; instead of their doing the job and Canterbury's paying its share, as with the police and fire brigade, this time Canterbury did the job and Kent paid, the whole arrangement being co-ordinated by a joint committee.

But while this was going on the great smear campaign against local government was so successful that function after function was being taken away. Memories are short; few seemed to remember the time when Hitler was at the gates, destruction rained from the sky, defeat was everywhere; when the army had escaped annihilation only by what was acknowledged as a miracle; the navy could only skulk at Scapa; when only The Few stood between defeat and capitulation. But the people, bombed night after night for months, stood cheerfully firm because they could see that somebody was doing something, and seemed to know what they were doing; and that 'somebody', though in the background it may have been the central government, in the foreground, visible to the citizens, was the local authority. Local government covered itself with glory in World War II, and for a time when peace was restored the attacks of the centralist critics subsided, but as the memories of local government's finest hour faded away, it became safe to resume the witch-hunt.

All this time Canterbury was fighting to keep up its standards; when the war ended, the great cry was for more houses; Canterbury built more per thousand population than any other county borough; then for more schools; in this small city a dozen or so were built. Tens of millions were spent; the manifold difficulties of rebuilding the war-damaged city were overcome successfully; the population was already increasing, and with it prosperity, when there came what was thought to be the culminating triumph; the university. Surely, people thought, Canterbury was now home and dry. It had acquitted itself worthily, while never allowing pride to interfere with efficiency, and had equipped itself with greater resource to ensure progress. It is a bitter turn of fate that if the intention was to safeguard the city's future status all this should turn out to have been a complete waste of time. If the city council had sat back and done nothing, it would have made no difference, for the same destiny of extinction —at least the government has been impartial—is suffered by every small and medium-sized town and city, and the same removal of every worthwhile power and authority is suffered by even the largest outside the concentrated industrial areas.

However, things could be worse, and may become better. The district in which Canterbury finds itself is one whose communications radiate from the city, and whose population look to it for shopping and many other services. The new unit—already in embryo existence—has decided to call itself 'Canterbury' and hopes, with Her Majesty's gracious help, to become a city and take over the custody of the old traditions. If this were to happen the result would not be too bad. Some people would have to adjust their outlook to accept a 'city' in which are vast tracts of open country, and urban settlements separated by country from the old city. This is only the converse of the adjustment that had to be made in 1835 when the rural tracts in the old liberties of the city were taken away; the adjustment may be greater in scale but the principle is the same. This means that the ancient city, if we regard it as a continuing conception, relies on the new inhabitants of the district, the people of Herne Bay and Whitstable and Bridge and Blean, to take on with pride the traditions for which the old city has fought so hard and so long. Surely she will not call on them in vain.

While we hope that the new dispensation will, in the end, show a satisfactory result, there is no earthly reason why the present city, perhaps with a moderate enlargement to take in overspill, could have not functioned as a district on its own. The violent changes that the Conservative government brought about would be more palatable if the scheme of 'reform' was likely to bring great benefit to the country as a whole. But one suspects that the only thing it has to commend it is that it may make life easier for civil servants and politicians—there will be less of that really genuine local democracy which can so disturb the slumbers of Whitehall and Westminster. From any other point of view it is 'simply crackers', 'terribly bad', 'indefensible gerrymandering', and 'hopelessly irrelevant'. That, at any rate, is how Baroness Sharp describes it. And as a former Permanent Secretary to the Ministry of Housing and Local Government she should know what she is talking about.

October 1973

BIBLIOGRAPHY

Babington, M., *The Romance of Canterbury Cathedral*, London: Raphael Tuck & Sons, 1932

Bamford and Bankes, *Vicious Circle*, London: Parish, 1965

Barham, Richard Harris, *The Ingoldsby Legends*, London: O.U.P., 1938

Bede, *Ecclesiastical History*, Everyman Edition, London: Dent, 1963

Boyle, J., *Canterbury Pilgrims' Guide*, Canterbury City Council, 1968

Bullock, E. H., *Planning To-morrow's Britain*, London: Frederick Muller, 1944

Bunce, Cyprian, *Minutes of Canterbury*, Canterbury: Kentish Gazette, 1800–01

Cantacuzino, Sherban, and others, *Canterbury, City Buildings Series*, London: Studio Vista, 1970

Chaucer, G., *The Canterbury Tales*, Oxford: Clarendon Press, 1894

Clapham, A. W., *English Romanesque Architecture before the Conquest*, Oxford: Clarendon Press, 1930

Collingwood and Myers, *Roman Britain and the English Settlements*, Oxford: Clarendon Press, 1949

Cotton, C., *The Grey Friars of Canterbury*, Manchester: University Press, 2nd ed., 1926

Cozens, Walter, *Old Canterbury*, Canterbury: Cross & Jackman, 1906

Defoe, Daniel, *A Tour through the Whole Island of Great Britain*, Everyman, London: Dent, 1948

Edwards, D. L., *History of the King's School, Canterbury*, London: Faber, 1957

Eliot, T. S., *Murder in the Cathedral*, London: Westminster Press, 1951

Everitt, A. M., *The Community of Kent and the Great Rebellion*, Leicester: University Press, 1966

Frere, S., *The Roman Theatre at Canterbury*, reprint from *Britannia*, Vol. 1, pp. 83–113, Canterbury Excavation Committee, 1970

Roman Canterbury, 4th edition, Canterbury Excavation Committe, 1965

Gardiner, D., *The Story of the English Towns, Canterbury*, London: Sheldon Press, 1950

Harris, Lord, *History of Kent County Cricket*, London: Eyre & Spottiswoode, 1907

Harvey, John H., *Henry Yevele*, London: Batsford, 1944

Hawkes, Jacquetta and Christopher, *Prehistoric Britain*, London: Penguin, 1947

Higenbottam, F., *The Apparition of Mrs. Veal, etc.*, reprint from *Archaeologia Cantiana*, Vol. LXXIII, pp. 154–166, 1959

Hilton, John, *The Canterbury and Whitstable Railway*, Hadlow, Kent: John Hilton Press, 1966

Jenkins, Claude, *The Life and Times of Cranmer*, Cathedral Papers No. 7, 1936

Jenkins, Frank, *Men of Kent before the Romans*, Canterbury Archaeological Society, 1962

Knowles, David, *Thomas Becket*, London: A. & C. Black, 1970
    Religious Orders in England, Cambridge University Press, 3 vols., 1955–9

Martin, A. R., *The Dominican Priory at Canterbury*, from *Archaeological Journal*, Vol. LXXXVI, pp. 152–77, 1929

Potts, R. U., *Plan of St. Augustine's Abbey, Canterbury*, Canterbury: St. Augustine's College, 1934

Rackham, Bernard, *The Ancient Glass of Canterbury Cathedral*, London: Lund Humphries, 1949

Taylor, Arthur F., *The Free Churches of Canterbury*, 1929

Tennyson, Alfred Lord, *Becket*, London: Macmillan, 1884

Urry, W. G., *Canterbury Under the Angevin Kings*, London: Athlone Press, 1967
    The Normans in Canterbury, Canterbury Archaeological Society, 1959

Willis, R., *Architectural History of Canterbury Cathedral*, London: Longman, etc., 1845
    History of the Monastery of Christ Church, Canterbury, *Archaeologia Cantiana*, Vol. VII, pp. 1–206, 1868

Woodruff and Danks, *Memorials of the Cathedral and Priory of Christ in Canterbury*, London: Chapman & Hall, 1912

INDEX

Abbot's Mill, 75, 118
Abbot's Barton, 123
Accord of Winchester, 49
Adam of Charing, 77
Aelfword, 73
Air raids (and precautions), 121, 128
Aldhun, 73
Alexander II, Pope, 63
Alexander of Gloucester, 77
All Saints Court, 111
All Souls College, Oxford, 89
Almshouses: John and Ann Smith's, 38;
  Sir Roger Manwood's, 156, 165;
  Jesus Hospital, 156
Alphege, St., 46, 93
Amenity societies, 161
American Bar Association, 177
Angevins, 52
Anne, Queen, 112
Anouilh, 65
Anselm, 49, 68, 115, 180
Antiquarians, 157
Archaeology: digging in 1944, 25;
  technique, 25, 26; dating material, 25;
  conditions in Canterbury, 26; in
  Westgate Gardens, 27; early Saxon
  huts, 45; cobbled yard *temp*. Alfred the
  Great, 45
Architecture, style of: 35; Gothic, 75; Per-
  pendicular, 86; proposed by Dr. Holden
  for rebuilding Canterbury, 131; Minis-
  try's hesitation over, 135; proposals for
  St. George's Street approved, 136; dis-
  pute over colonnade in St. George's
  Street, 136–7, 140; St. Augustine's
  College, 144; St. Edmund's School, 144
Archives, 158–9
Archivists, 157–8
Around Canterbury, places of interest,
  175–7
Art, Canterbury College of, 147
Augustinian friary, 78
Austen, Jane, 175
Australians (cricket), 172

Babington, Margaret, 168
Baedeker raids, 127
Bailiffs, 72, 82
Baker, John, 171
Baldwin, Archbishop, 148
Bank of England, 46
Baptists, 117, 118
Bargrave, Dean, 103
Bargrave, Mrs., 111–13

Barham, R. H., 51, 58
Barnet, Battle of, 95
Barracks, 12
Bat-and-Trap, 168–9
Battely, Nicholas, 157
Bayeux Tapestry, 51
Beachy Head, 176
Beaney, The (Royal Museum and Beaney
  Institute), 17*ff*.; display of eulogy of
  city by John Twyne, 108; citizens'
  meeting in 1949, 134; F. Bennett-
  Goldney appointed honorary director,
  122
Beaney, Dr. James George, 18
Becket, Thomas, 60–9, 70, 71, 160; sister,
  Rohesia, 71
Bede, The Venerable, 32*ff*.
Bedford, Duke of, 139
Belgae, 24
Bell, Dean, 116
Bell Harry, 10, 11, 12, 84
Bennett-Goldney, Francis, 122–6, 139,
  158, 159
Bertha, Queen of Kent, 32, 38, 40
Beverley (Beverlie) Inn, 155, 156
Bigberry, 23
Bill of Rights, The, 164
Binyon, Laurence, 168
Blackfriars, 78, 79, 80, 99, 117
Black Prince, The, 89–90
Black Prince's Chantry, 100
Bluberd the Hermit, 94; execution, 158
Bluecoat School, 77, 108, 156
Bocking, Dr., 98
Boleyn, Anne, 98
Boys, Sir John, 156
Boyne, Battle of the, 164
Brent, John, 125
Breton, Richard le, 62, 63
Bribery, 126
Bridewell, 77
Bridge-Blean, 181
Bridges, Mrs., 115
Britons, 23
Broad Street, 36, 37, 42, 127
Bronze Age, 22
Brotherhood farm, 49
Bruman, 74
Buffs, The: Military museum in Poor
  Priests' Hospital, 77; Warriors' chapel
  as shrine of, 87; origins, 101; other
  titles, 101; association with Canterbury,
  101; ceremony in Warriors' Chapel,
  156; 179